*THE
INVESTIGATOR*

THE INVESTIGATOR

A Practical Guide to Private Detection

James E. Ackroyd

FREDERICK MULLER

First published in Great Britain 1974
by Frederick Muller Limited

Copyright © 1974 by James E. Ackroyd

All rights reserved. No part of this publication may be reproduced, stored in a retrieval system, or transmitted, in any form or by any means, electronic, mechanical, photocopying, recording or otherwise, without the prior permission of Frederick Muller Limited.

ISBN 0 584 10133 3

Printed in Great Britain by
Clarke, Doble & Brendon Ltd, Plymouth, Devon

Contents

	FOREWORD	7
1.	Introduction	11
2.	A Brief History	19
3.	Tracing Enquiries	22
4.	Missing Persons	26
5.	Interviews and Interrogation of Witnesses or Suspects	32
6.	Cautions	36
7.	Statements, Reports and Identification	39
8.	Matrimonial Enquiries—Adultery	57
9.	Criminal Investigations	71
10.	Industrial Espionage	79
11.	General Security Measures	81
12.	Giving Evidence	90
13.	Laws of Evidence and Procedure	96
14.	Service of Legal Process	102
15.	Commencing in Business	107
16.	Conclusion	119

Foreword

In spite of the general public interest in private detection, I am not aware of any other book ever being published which has attempted to cover the whole complex subject from beginning to end, even to the extent of providing information on procuring clients, starting up a business and dealing with administration. There have been various books touching on detective agencies and millions of thriller novels, but it seems that never before has a book actually been written with the express purpose of teaching the reader how to become a member of this rather specialized fraternity, and how to cope in practice with all assignments of the type encountered.

I do not claim to be a professional writer, merely someone who has spent the whole of his adult life in police and private investigation work, and as such I feel perhaps better qualified to explain in straightforward, everyday language the practical and theoretical knowledge which one must possess before this occupation can be even contemplated. I may be wrong, but I cannot possibly see how anyone could write a book on this wide subject without having had first-hand experience of the occupation.

Throughout the book I have not only taken great pains to instruct the reader as to how he should carry out all the varied duties, but have also endeavoured to point out the potential errors and pitfalls, together with enough illustrative experiences and examples to make the contents interesting as well as to communicate a practical knowledge of the subject.

Employment in this sphere is not restricted to males, nor indeed has it to be practised on a full-time basis. Almost every detective agency in the country engages at least a small part-time staff, and any man or woman possessing some knowledge of the business will be welcomed into their ranks. The work is extremely interesting, often involving excitement and travel and the remuneration can be very high.

This book should enable the reader to open his or her own agency, or supply the potential private investigator with enough knowledge to obtain a good post with an established firm. It should also prove informative reading for the journalistic profession, members of the police and persons working in similar fields, or those merely with an interest in the subject.

My first draft of this book ran to over four hundred pages, in which I tried to explain the vast and complicated subject of the Statute Law of England. This resulted in so many over-simplifications that it became obvious to me that I had tried to embark upon an impossible task. This book makes no attempt to accomplish this, but is aimed to help, educate and interest Private Investigators and other readers of every nation throughout the world. If it succeeds in this—and I sincerely feel that it should—then my endeavours have been justified.

J.E.A.

Note

All the firms, incidents and persons mentioned herein are imaginary and do not relate to any particular firm or incident, nor to any person, either living or dead. They are based on my personal experience over many years and are merely hypothetical illustrations.

J.E.A.

1
Introduction

To become proficient and find employment in this occupation is more difficult than one would imagine because apart from the very large detective agencies—some being public companies—the majority are small concerns employing few staff. In fact, one of the most difficult problems in a detective agency is obtaining suitably trained staff. A layman would immediately jump to the conclusion that the retiring police officer or police detective could adequately fill these posts. However, this is not always the case, although such experience would help a prospective student with court procedure and the criminal type of investigation to some degree. In fact the world of the police detective and the private detective are miles apart and in spite of their television image, there is seldom any need to work together. In some countries there may even be a certain hostility felt by the police towards private investigators, but fortunately this is rare.

The main difference between police and private investigators is their approach to a problem. The police have extensive official resources and backing, whereas the private investigator often relies only on his initiative and personality to succeed. Added to this are the two different types of work which, with exceptions, could briefly be classified thus: Police—Criminal, Private Investigator—Civil. Another great difference is that the private investigator must not only be a good detective, he must also be a good businessman. Experienced private investigators are very hard to find, whereas in the legal profession or accountancy a vacancy can be filled from a host of suitably qualified applicants, in the private investigation field it is often difficult to find a fitting employee and sometimes impossible.

One frequently has to be satisfied with second best and then a long period of training ensues.

Before becoming a private investigator one must get the work in the right perspective so that one's illusions are not shattered at a later date.

It is not a 9 a.m. to 5 p.m. occupation and anyone who is not prepared to work long, hard hours might as well give up at this stage. Obviously time can be made for recreation, but a good deal of the work involves late observations, interviewing suspects or witnesses at evenings or weekends, and sometimes it might even be necessary to work all night and still be in court next day to give evidence in some earlier case. In many countries the police detective does this sort of thing for no extra pay—or a mere pittance—whereas these extra hours mean more pay or higher profits to the private detective.

Probably the most advantageous aspect of private investigating is that it is seldom boring. It is one of the few occupations that offers the best of both worlds, problems to sustain the intellect, enough excitement to keep life interesting, together with excellent remuneration.

This occupation is no longer limited to the male for throughout the world there are numerous women heading successful agencies, and almost all firms of substance now acknowledge their equality with men. In some enquiries they are indispensible, e.g. under cover in a gown store or other female section, but apart from these obvious instances—ignoring the feminine habit of marriage and children—they make equally excellent operatives.

Many inquiries are out of the city from which an investigator operates. This entails either instructing a detective agency in that area, or travelling to the place and carrying out the assignment personally. However, as the client often prefers his own detective to deal with the case, there are good opportunities for someone who enjoys travelling to spend as much as a third of his life in different parts of the country, with an occasional trip abroad.

One myth continually heard within the investigation field is 'born detective' or 'born policeman', which is utterly misleading and illogical. The only way to become a first-class detective is by attaining a good general knowledge of both criminal and civil laws of the country through lectures and books; by obtaining practical experience in court work, perhaps working for an agency part-time, reading books on investigation work, especially those recounting specific cases and one might even consider joining the local police. This book will certainly supply much information required to commence in business, even down to advice about administration and its obvious pitfalls, but it cannot endow the reader with three of the most important attributes; the ability to work hard, absolute integrity and sound common sense.

It may be that you are not thinking in the terms of full-time employment, but simply as a means of obtaining sufficient knowledge to acquire an interesting and remunerative spare-time occupation. Much of the routine work of every detective agency can be dealt with on this basis, and few other callings pay so generously or adapt so well to spare-time labours. It could be argued that it would be much safer to begin a new occupation in this manner, collecting experience and saving for the future. On the other hand, working only evenings and weekends, one is almost certain to miss the really big assignments. No one could possibly give any advice on this problem as the decision must always rest with the individual and his own particular qualifications, financial circumstances and ambitions.

As an interesting aside to give some idea of the potential earning power, let us suppose for a moment that you have read this book and wish to become a spare-time investigator. Work is obtained from one law firm, acting as their process server, i.e. one who delivers legal documents, usually associated in some manner with court actions, and you 'serve' only five or six per week. This will seldom present any problems, and yet the fees involved will usually increase an average man's income by about 30 per cent before tax. This is private investigation work on a really minute scale, but it will be seen by this illustration that the return is very handsome. In addition, other types of work easily managed by the spare-time man are surveillance, 'skip' tracing and status reports.

Whether you start up in business on your own, work for an agency full-time or just indulge on a part-time basis, do not begin to speak or act like a 'James Bond' character. This is an occupation which might sometimes have its exciting moments, but a false, childish veneer will only arouse feeling of distrustful unease in your clients and your bank balance will suffer. Always be natural, work hard and the clients will feel confident that their problems are being dealt with correctly.

It is also very important to be regarded as a dependable and trustworthy investigator by individual law firms because many of the assignments will originate from the same source. The secret is to make sure that all the existing clients are retained, and as time passes many more are added by recommendation and advertising. In this way the business will prosper. Many people use that fateful expression 'when one door closes another opens', shrugging their shoulders philosophically when another client is lost. This is an impractical attitude to adopt, since in the end all doors will be well and truly closed. Even though apparently impossible, the aim at least should be to retain every client.

Advertising will presumably attract private clients and it is equally important that their interests are conscientiously pursued. In practice, the private clients supply an agency with many of its more interesting and higher paid assignments, but it must never be forgotten that the law firms supply the regular day-to-day work of the private investigator and thus, to some extent, they do deserve precedence over everyone else.

There will be times when even the most experienced investigator will not properly understand a certain problem. Good advice here is to put pride on one side and either telephone or see the law firm for elucidation. If the instructions are from a private client then contact your most friendly solicitor for guidance. As much of the work involves legal matters it is essential not to make mistakes. Should this occur, do not under any circumstances try to blunder on, bluff it out or deny something, as the mistake is almost sure to be revealed at some stage and it is far better to admit the fault, apologizing profusely. In most cases it can then be rectified without too much loss of face.

A good proportion of all detective agency work will be in handling matrimonial enquiries, security, criminal investigations, tracing missing persons and the service of legal process. The work of any agency can be so varied that they are constantly dealing with intricate problems for the first time and it is here that common sense is really essential. It is said that a private detective agency is 'more interested in restitution than prosecution', but this must not be taken too literally and great care must be employed to ensure that the investigator himself is not guilty of an offence. The returning of stolen goods is not an offence but there may be accompanying circumstances which create an offence, e.g. where stolen goods are returned on the condition that 'no prosecution ensues'. Every investigator should look with great care at this hypothesis and discover exactly how it relates to himself. In Great Britain it is a definite offence known as Compounding a Felony.

It is worthwhile being on the friendliest of terms with other investigators in the area as many hours of boring routine can often be saved by a regular exchange of information, particularly in the case of tracing enquiries. Since many firms are usually looking for the same person, especially with debt tracings, an ideal situation would be for every agency to circularize every successful trace.

Report writing is dealt with later in the book, but certain basic rules always apply to both reports and letters. In both documents one should be extremely careful not to include any slander or libellous matter within the text. Never state something as a fact when it is really an opinion, and if tempted to make a slanderous opinion, say nothing at all. This may not apply as significantly when sending a report or letter to an instructing law firm as they understand the position, but to do this with a law firm acting for the other side or a private client, would be sheer folly. At some stage the wording would almost certainly be shown to the person named and serious trouble might then ensue. If the report or letter is factual and can be proved, then providing the recipient has a right to know, it is in order for the document to be sent. Study very carefully your country's law with regard to Slander and Libel.

After being in business for some time, or even at the outset, it is advisable to join a recognized detective association in order to have agents in all parts of your own country and abroad. There will usually be various choices, but before obtaining membership ensure that they are a reputable, well established organization, able to supply lists of agents throughout the world. This is one of the main advantages of membership, although it is also possible to receive a considerable amount of work from other members. The best associations also provide injury and sickness benefits.

AGENCY WORK

When enquiries are received from agents it is customary to work at a lower fee, ensuring that they also gain from the transaction. If no intimation of the proposed fee is apparent in the instructing letter it is much wiser to sort this problem out before commencing the work. Conversely, when instructing an agent always inform him of the approximate fee so that he can assess the limit of his labours, which prevents unnecessary disputes later. Bear in mind that when an agent is instructed, even if the client defaults, you are honour-bound to pay the agent. The obvious rule then is to be sure of the client before instructing an agent, perhaps obtaining the whole fee or at least a substantial deposit in advance. However, each case should be judged individually for if the client is known or happens to be a well respected businessman, he may feel insulted by your obvious lack of trust.

PRIVATE CLIENTS

One further word of warning relating to the attitude of private clients towards success and failure. If everything falls into place and an enquiry is completely successful the matter usually warrants congratulations, possibly even a bonus, and the account is settled immediately. These cases are often comparatively easy, not really warranting any special merit. The other side of this story is the investigation which is fraught with complications, untold hours are devoted to it and every avenue explored but nothing proves successful, and eventually defeat has to be admitted. When this happens, although there may have been treble the amount of work and thought expended, the client may refuse to pay, obviously considering the investigator incompetent. Due to the abortive results the account has probably been reduced anyway, but if no compromise is reached the investigator has no option but to seek vindication through the courts. Fortunately this is an exception to the rule but it does happen and can be most unpleasant. If an enquiry seems to be taking this course it is wiser to immediately curtail work and warn the client, thereby putting the onus on him as to whether or not he is prepared to authorize further expenditure.

Detective agencies often have their lighter moments. I can recall quite vividly an August afternoon some time ago when I was disturbed from quietly checking reports by the buzzing intercom. Reception announced that a Mr X wished to see me urgently and the girl stressed that he would only consult the principal as the matter was of such a delicate and confidential nature.

As this sort of preliminary discourse invariably typified a matrimonial case, I was tempted to re-direct the call to an employee, but since it had been such a calm, uninteresting day I decided to relieve the monotony by seeing him.

A tall, well-dressed individual of about fifty was shown into the office. At first sight he had the appearance of being a professional man or someone of importance. As he sat down in the armchair beside my desk I wondered cynically—a hazard of the profession—what dilemma had compelled him to seek our services. Was his wife having an affair with the refuse collector? Perhaps his daughter had run off with an unwashed, penniless good-for-nothing! He appeared to have substantial means and mentally I had already added him to my list of lucrative private clients. As usual, I contrived to look sympathetically interested, relaxing into my swivel chair, pen poised, so that every syllable should be recorded.

Glancing up I noticed Mr X fidgeting, craning his neck and darting furtive glances about the office. Mildly alarmed, I gave a swift look around but could see nothing to explain his strange behaviour. No longer relaxed, I said 'Is something wrong?'

'Wrong?' he shouted piercingly. 'Wrong? Yes, there is something wrong. He is going to kill me.' His head dropped forward on to his hands, uncontrollable sobs wracked his body and tears trickled through his fingers.

The quiet summer afternoon of a few moments ago had reverted in seconds to something ugly and dangerous.

Mr X eventually calmed down and I felt it time he furnished an explanation to justify the outburst. I was also feeling a little uneasy about his undisciplined behaviour and began to suspect that he might be mentally unstable. Giving him the benefit of my doubts I said, 'If someone is threatening to kill you, surely the obvious people to see are the police?'

He leaned towards me confidentially, his words resolving all my doubts. 'The police do not believe me. If I go again they will send me back to the mental home. What can I do? My next door neighbour sends nuclear rays into my bedroom and I am getting radio-active. . . .' The man was crazy.

As he rambled on, my paramount thought was how to get rid of the poor wretch. I could ask him to leave or have him thrown out, but I was loath to use either method. In a flash of inspiration my Machiavellian resourcefulness came to the rescue and, mentally congratulating myself on the sly subtlety of it, I wrote down the name and address of my main competitor. I handed this to Mr X, saying, 'I should see this gentleman, he specializes in nuclear rays.'

To which Mr X retorted, 'I just came from there and he told me you were the expert!'

2
A Brief History

The bulk of detective agencies are quite properly regarded as respectable business enterprises, but this was not always so. One may hear private investigators spoken of in rather derogatory terms and this attitude seems to originate from the founder members of the occupation. The first private investigators had a terrible reputation, being utterly unscrupulous in their dealings and little more than confidence tricksters. Whilst their status is now impeccable, they are still misjudged by a fast diminishing minority who are loath to recognize that today's versatile private investigator performs many needed functions in our modern society.

The launching of this profession in Great Britain was just before or during the Victorian era (1837–1901) and most agencies were in and around London.

It is not surprising that these agencies had a vile reputation as the majority were in existence merely to supply a cover for their illegal activities of supplying prostitutes to anyone who could afford them; a type of yesteryear call-girl system. These girls also came in useful for arranged divorces. Many of the 'detectives' had criminal records and some could neither read nor write. It seems incredible that such ignoramuses of this calibre should be entrusted with confidential matters and, not surprisingly, they took advantage of this trust. A favourite trick was to obtain divorce evidence, but instead of taking it back to their client, it would be offered to the guilty party for a price; in other words, blackmail.

Divorce in the early days was a rare thing compared with today, very much restricted to the upper income groups. The overall fee could be up to a thousand pounds and the investigator's fee was also much higher.

At this time there was another type of agency coming into being, specializing not in detection but in the prevention of crime. In effect, these were privately hired police forces used to carry out security patrols, particularly in the dock area of London. They were really glorified night watchmen who were badly paid. Between these two kinds of agency there was very little to enhance the reputation of the private investigator.

In America things were vastly different and detective agencies were gaining a firm hold in the field of prevention and detection of crime. One of the better and oldest established organizations was formed in 1852 by an ex-Glaswegian, Allen Pinkerton, and called Pinkerton's International Detective Agency. They had a very efficient department for the detection of crime but their main source of revenue came from the private army of 'toughs' used by the industrialists of that era for breaking up large mobs of strikers. This firm is now a public company regularly producing million dollar profits for the shareholders each year.

With certain exceptions, even today the American detective agencies are run on a much larger scale than their counterparts overseas. They still have the one-man agencies, but in the main detective agencies in America have become big business and are a recognized part of normal commercial life. For instance, the majority of factories or other business premises would seldom hire their own security staff; a detective agency would supply uniformed guards for an annual retainer. Nor would the responsibility of the agency end there. Usually an expert operative of the agency would visit the premises and make a security survey, submitting plans and a written report to the executive board outlining the weaknesses in security and offering helpful advice and suggestions to remedy these defects, together with the approximate cost involved. As these reports are often acted upon, the crime figures for breaking offences in the United States are much lower than they might otherwise be. In Britain and in other countries there are similar organizations, but as yet they have not gained a proper foothold in the business world due to a general lack of interest in the involved subject of security.

However, the detective in other countries has also progressed since those early days and one or more agencies can usually be found in every city on this side of the Iron Curtain. A few investigators still work from home, perhaps an ex-policeman trying to eke out his pension, and in most cases they are quite competent to tackle a matrimonial tangle, but they are not properly equipped to deal with the more formidable assignments. A more organized, businesslike investigator is coming to the fore and the quicker the complete changeover takes place the better. If a detective agency is to supply an adequate and efficient service at all times it should be situated in business premises and conducted along normal business lines.

The purpose of this book, however, is to enable would-be private investigators to achieve a high standard, and none of the foregoing comments exclude the part-time or one-man agency from obtaining lucrative rewards from the occupation. As things stand at the moment the majority of detective work is carried out on this basis, but the profession is wide open for new blood and modern business methods. We have supermarkets, nuclear weapons, supersonic air travel and numerous other exciting modern innovations, but many private investigators still carry on with the same old methods and make no progress whatever.

3
Tracing Enquiries

Some explanation is required here as at first sight, the two designations, Tracing and Missing Persons (see next chapter), seem to be so similar as to be identical. However, in practice, this is not the case and it should be stressed that these differ greatly in their relative importance. Broadly speaking a tracing enquiry is a debtor who has moved without leaving a forwarding address and who can usually be found without too much trouble, for a small fee. A missing person enquiry is usually quite a serious matter, requiring urgent attention and the fee is dependent on the amount of work involved, but it is usually quite high. There are always exceptions to any rule and all cases must be treated on their individual merits. For instance, if a creditor disappeared owing a tremendous debt, the enquiry would warrant the urgency and labour of a missing person investigation together with the appropriate fee. On the other hand, if the fee was limited on a missing person enquiry—usually not because of greed but through lack of funds—take the job on but work it in with other assignments; do not circulate descriptions or photographs, and keep expenditure as low as possible. It would be very important in this instance to explain that instructions could only be accepted on this basis.

Like many other occupations, some work will not add any monetary gain to the balance sheet. In fact on an individual trace or some other minute enquiry there will often be a definite loss. These small losses must be taken philosophically as one cannot expect regular clients to pass instructions on larger and more profitable assignments if the investigator is not prepared to undertake the smaller and less attractive aspects of the job. It is very important in any work appertaining to the legal profession to have the right attitude towards this problem from the very outset since it so frequently occurs. One must be fair with a solicitor who supplies an abundance of work but is limited on this small enquiry. The same vein seems to continue throughout the legal profession; for instance a legal firm receives excellent fees for conveying property but may spend the best part of a day in the local court on a debt matter for a ridiculously low fee.

For regular clients who supply the agency with a quantity of work, or a new firm you hope will become a regular client, treat them fairly and if the situation warrants it, be prepared to work at a loss. Do not grumble about this or, on the other hand, be nauseatingly magnanimous, just do it quietly in good grace and you will find it greatly appreciated. Situations like these are golden opportunities to build up goodwill. However, never work at a loss for a private client.

Every agency deals with hundreds of tracing enquiries each year, usually coming from law firms or finance houses who have written or commenced proceedings but then discovered that the debtor had moved, without leaving a forwarding address.

There is no standard procedure for receiving instructions. They may be by telephone or a brief letter giving the name and previous address of the defaulter. Remember, this is a small enquiry so do not make a big investigation out of it; there is no need for descriptions or photographs.

When in the area, call at the previous address and ask the present occupiers if they know the new address of the previous occupants. The usual answer will be negative, but sometimes it produces the new address or at least a street or an area. Sometimes the people have not moved at all, but have themselves returned the letter to your clients marked 'Gone Away' or 'Not known at this address', in order to avoid payment of the debt. This is the exception but it does happen.

See the neighbours on either side and it is most likely that one of them will know the new address. If not, ask who were their particular friends in the neighbourhood and also where the male inhabitant or any member of the family work. Never be officious or co-operation will not be forthcoming. A polite and pleasant attitude will usually elicit the information quite easily. Children often know the new address of their friends and are only too willing to talk.

Should the employers of the debtor or family be known, either write to the welfare officer or company secretary enclosing a stamped addressed envelope, or alternatively make a personal call asking to see the debtor. When interviewed simply ask for their present address.

It may be possible to visit a bar which the debtor frequents or contact the firm who carried out the removal; any information of this type is extremely useful. If any of the family are involved in any way with an official department it may be possible to obtain the new address from this source.

Remember, it is only necessary to obtain one of these leads and in practice it will be found that the next door neighbour can usually supply this.

ALWAYS VERIFY THE NEW ADDRESS. This only takes a few minutes when in the area and is ABSOLUTELY ESSENTIAL. It often happens that someone supplies the new address in good faith but genuinely makes a mistake, calling the road an avenue or grove, or giving the wrong number. Upon being notified of the new address the client will usually incur quite substantial costs in the issue of some legal proceedings, and if the address is wrong, money has been wasted and the investigator appears very incompetent.

There are many ways to trace people but, because of the low fee, a successful result must be arrived at with a minimum of labour and time. Tracings can be done whilst already in the area, and the new address can await verification until the new area is visited. In this way the work is carried out in a few minutes with no actual expenditure. It is a good idea to keep the tracing enquiries with you the whole time, for these tend to build up in the office and it may sometimes be advisable, in the interests of efficiency, to work a full day or so to clear them up. Many will be in the same area and it is possible to have quite a profitable day. On the other hand, if they had been completed along with other work, the same money would have been earned with no loss of valuable time.

Should an address be traced to some distant town, write to the clients explaining this but point out that it has not actually been verified. Before incurring any costs they will then be able to write for confirmation. It is better that they write as the investigator may not be aware of the reason why the new address is required and a letter might cause confusion.

During enquiries, the questions are often asked about who requires the information, but never discuss a person's business with anyone else. It is sufficient to say that the information is needed on behalf of solicitors or clients, without saying anything further. The same answer will suffice when actually verifying the address with the persons concerned. Even if the purpose is known it is always wisest to plead ignorance.

Unless absolutely necessary it is better to ask questions on the doorstep, otherwise a good deal of valuable time will be wasted. This does not necessarily apply to other enquiries as it can be most beneficial to spend time gaining the confidence of the other party.

At different times various instructions may be received to trace the same person and it is therefore wise to carefully file every enquiry for future reference. Upon receiving subsequent enquiries the new address must again be verified. The bad debtor population of any city is always on the move and the same people have to be traced time and time again. This is why cooperation with other agencies can be most helpful.

FEES

These vary in different parts of the world, but the lowest fee would be for law firms who supply the more profitable work. If urgency is required it would be feasible to charge more but as a rule there is no desperate rush.

For other clients who only send tracing enquiries, the charge must be much higher or a regular loss will be sustained.

An unsuccessful trace must have a fully detailed report on the extent of enquiries and the account should be kept to a minimum, whereas only a short letter is needed if the enquiry is successful.

4
Missing Persons

This is a very complex and important enquiry, usually involving a tremendous amount of painstaking routine and a good deal of initial administration before a result can be achieved. Usually they originate from private clients and are often of such an urgent nature that it may be advisable temporarily to put all other work on one side in order to concentrate wholeheartedly on this one case. These are the more remunerative types of enquiry and therefore one should be prepared to work accordingly. If the assignment looks very difficult it will obviously involve the agency in a good deal of expenditure. If the client appears unreliable, get a substantial deposit at the outset.

The client can obviously come from any walk of life, and as cruel as it may seem, the investigation must be dealt with bearing this in mind. It might be quite in order to work on a very small profit margin if sympathy is felt towards someone, or even take weekly instalments, but never lose sight of the fact that basically you are in business to make money. One sees many unfortunate and often heartbreaking incidents in a detective agency where someone badly needs assistance but cannot afford it. In these circumstances only the individual investigator can decide what course to follow.

Missing persons can be either domestic, e.g. wives, etc., or criminal, e.g. company directors who have absconded with funds, but basically the methods used will be more or less the same. All the enquiries appertaining to tracings apply equally to missing persons but here the investigation is taken much further. The client may sometimes be reluctant to have the neighbours questioned and unless his attitude changes it could be a hindrance to the whole assignment. This should be pointed out but if the client insists the investigator has no option but to accede. If this is felt to be badly hampering the investigation, approach the client again on the subject.

Apart from the above exception, it must be remembered that all the previous comments with regard to tracing enquiries apply even more stringently in a missing person investigation, the only difference being that one would not try to cut corners or avoid entering neighbours' houses.

Success or failure will depend very largely on the extent and precision of the original instructions received from the client. If sufficient facts are not obtained the enquiry will soon lapse from lack of leads and the whole thing will be a complete but costly farce. We all know that the client can be asked a few further questions, but if the maximum information is not secured at the first interview, all the same people will have to be seen again once further details have been revealed in the subsequent interview. When seen at the initial meeting the client is usually over-anxious and because of this he may try to take over the interview. In these circumstances the investigator would probably glean a few basic facts, but insufficient to carry out the enquiry effectively.

The best way to take instructions is first to let the client tell his story in his own way and then to conduct an interview on a question and answer basis, taking extensive notes on the points covered. Never try to commit details to memory as this is absolutely fatal. Record every single item of information because, although it may not appear to have any bearing on the subject at that stage, it may have great significance at a later date.

Obtain a good portrait photograph of the missing person, a description of the clothes worn when last seen and also a description of clothes taken away.

A very full and detailed personal description, in accordance with the following questionnaire, would be needed.

1. Place of birth.
2. Date of birth (if known) or age (apparent).
3. Occupation (any known previous occupation to be included).
4. Height.
5. Build (stout, medium, thin, erect, stooping, etc.).
6. Face (long, round, broad, smiling, sullen, wrinkled, etc.).
7. Complexion (fair, dark, pale, sallow, fresh, make-up, etc.).

8. Clean shaven or facial hair (colour, quantity, style).
9. Hair (colour, quantity, parting, style, waved, bleached or dyed).
10. Forehead (high, low, bulging, straight, receding, etc.).
11. Eyebrows (colour, thick, thin, shape, pencilled, plucked, etc.).
12. Eyes (colour, large, small, squint, peculiarities, glasses).
13. Nose (large, small, hook, straight, flat, broken, turned up).
14. Mouth (large, small, open, closed, droop at corners).
15. Lips (thick, thin, upper or lower protruding, pale, etc.).
16. Teeth (white, discoloured, prominent, gaps, dentures, etc.).
17. Chin (receding, projecting, dimpled, double, etc.).
18. Ears (large, small, close to head, protruding, pierced, long or short lobes).
19. Distinguishing marks (scars, warts, birthmarks, pimples, tattoos etc.).
20. Peculiarities (stammer, accent, gait, deformities, etc.).
21. Habits (fond of racing, games, smoking, drinking, opposite sex, speaks of .... etc.).
22. Dress.

A sample of handwriting may come in useful at some later stage of the inquiry and also a full description of the car, including year and registration number.

It is not unknown for titled or well known members of wealthy families to stay at hotels under an assumed name. If this should be the case, ascertain what aliases have been used in the past. If the missing person is a married woman, make sure that her maiden name is noted for it is very common practice for a missing wife to revert to it.

Get a complete list of all friends and relatives, break it down into those who are nearest and most popular and those who are barely remembered or merely acquaintances.

Bear in mind that

when people decide to disappear, although they might discuss it with a near relation or good friend, they often decide to keep all close relationships at bay, preferring to discuss their problems with a comparative outsider. In spite of this, the first enquiries should be made with the more obvious relatives and friends.

Make a complete list of recent associations, as the key to the whole situation can often be discovered from this source.

A comprehensive list of favourite holiday resorts, or a place they have always talked about visiting and find out if their passport is missing. Try to ascertain how much money was taken, and the bank should be checked, particularly the joint account. Ask if they have disappeared before. If so, what did they do and where did they go. If they previously ran away with someone else, the name and address of that person should be obtained and should be the first place visited.

An unpleasant question, but one which should be asked, is whether the person has ever talked about or contemplated suicide. If suicide or foul play is suspected, the police should be informed. This would not, however, exclude the investigator from continuing the enquiry.

A careful note should be taken of when the client last saw the missing person, and what took place at that time. Get an opinion as to the state of mind and ask if there is any history of mental illness.

If there has been an association with someone who has also disappeared, then all the relevant questions in relation to their disappearance will have to be gone into for a second time with the respective family. This is presuming that they have gone away together. In this case the investigation is easier since it doubles the amount of possible leads.

If the missing person is related to the client, they will be able to supply all the initial information. On the other hand should the missing person be an employee or someone not connected with the client, it will be necessary to visit the nearest relatives to obtain most of the required details.

Do not forget that the client is closest to the problem, and that he has probably been thinking of nothing else since it happened. He may have formulated some excellent ideas which might be very useful.

Always feel satisfied that you are not being innocently used for a criminal purpose, e.g. a criminal trying to trace his blackmail victim. This has happened but is very exceptional.

It is impossible to point out every question which should be asked in this type of enquiry as it is impossible to envisage every situation which could arise. The investigator must pursue an individual course on each enquiry and apply the contents of this chapter where relevant, but he must also be prepared to formulate further questions to reveal information which is particularly pertinent to the given set of circumstances.

Be quite clear at the very outset what action the client requires when the person is found. Usually, in the case of domestic disappearances, the client will prefer to contact the subject alone. In other cases he may want the investigator to deal with it, or perhaps accompany him, particularly where funds have gone astray, in which case the enquiry would not be over but would in fact require a good deal of further attention.

When all the details outlined in this and the previous chapter have been ascertained, plus any others which may arise, the actual work can begin.

ACTION REQUIRED

The course of action prescribed will be based on the assumption that the client is prepared to pay a substantial fee, enabling the exploration of every avenue to obtain a successful result. It must be stressed that one could not possibly carry out all the following enquiries if the fee was limited. The first economy would be to dispense with the compilation and distribution of circulars and photographs. It may also be found that the only way to deal economically with the matter is to treat it more or less as an ordinary enquiry.

The first step would be to send the photograph away for two or three hundred prints to be made, depending on how many agents and others are to be circularized. It is advisable to have an arrangement with a local photographer who is prepared to cooperate and do this type of work immediately.

Next see the residence last occupied by the abscondee, in the hope that some information can be revealed as to the destination or possible associate, e.g. travel brochure or letters. Whilst there it would be advisable to have a quick word with the neighbours to try to elicit the time of departure and mode of transport, e.g. taxi, private car. (You would later attempt to trace the taxi driver or get a full description of the private car and occupants.)

Without further delay return to the office and, based on the relevant facts, compile a detailed letter in the form of a duplicated circular, which should be posted immediately, together with a photograph, to all agents. The circular should contain every possible detail and must also point out that the circular is not a letter of instruction, but simply a request for their cooperation whilst conducting other duties. However, do say that in the event of any worthwhile lead, disbursements and normal fees would be forthcoming. Also ask them to regard the circular as current until cancelled. If the missing person is found, a short polite cancellation should be circularized. If some idea is known of the destination, then more specific instructions might be sent to agents in that area, unless you are going yourself. If a car is involved, a circular to the chief automobile association patrol office and road breakdown service would not be amiss.

Once satisfied that all the administrative side of the enquiry is under way then start attacking the problem in earnest. The file will already have grown with the progress chart, the original instructions which might well run to four or five pages of longhand notes, the sample of handwriting, the circular, and a typewritten report on your visit to the house and neighbours. The dossier should be constantly fed with new reports until at the end it shows a full and complete record outlining the whole investigation. Each report should contain the name and address of the interviewee, the information received and at the bottom there should be two designations, firstly the time involved and secondly the miles travelled.

The whole enquiry now depends entirely on the ability of the independent investigator. It is up to him to follow up all the various leads and handle the interviews tactfully, gathering together sufficient further information to eventually trace the missing person.

There are often various short cuts to obtain information and these are frequently overlooked in the heat of the investigation. For instance, looking up a name in a classified or trade directory, or telephone directory, advertising for information in the national or local press; contacting insurance companies where a policy is in force; asking their solicitor if aware of his address to forward a letter. This last instance warns them, but circumstances may warrant this action.

FEES

As always, these will vary in different parts of the world but the final fee is usually arrived at by an hourly or daily rate, plus hire of car, mileage and disbursements, e.g. agents' fees, printing, overnight expenses and meals.

5
Interviews and Interrogation of Witnesses or Suspects

In every enquiry there is someone who can give useful information and such persons have usually to be diligently sought out and the required details extracted from them. They themselves will probably begin an interview by telling the investigator that they are unable to help as they know nothing, being unaware of the value of the small details that they know. They say this quite honestly but can often be of great assistance.

Interrogation cannot really be taught in a book or anywhere else, but can only be acquired by experience. However, some of the main points to remember are these:

1. Adopt a correct, friendly, natural and tactful manner when approaching a witness. Do not be too official.
2. Consider beforehand, where possible, what information you hope to gain from the person.
3. Put the interviewee at ease and talk over the subject before committing anything to writing.
4. Where necessary, record the information received in the form of a statement. This only applies to actual witnesses; in the case of general enquiries a pocketbook entry will suffice.
5. If possible interview the person alone, the presence of a third party often causes tension and embarrassment.
6. With important enquiries do not interview people standing on the doorstep or in a bar. See them comfortably seated in their own home, at the office or even in a motor car. If useful information is hoped for they must feel at ease. There is always the exception, but this should be the general rule.
7. Never underestimate the person being interviewed. If any attempt

is made to obtain information by shady and outrageous methods they may well realize this and refuse to cooperate. Different situations require different approaches, but it will be found that an honest approach is by far the best and most rewarding.
8. If the statement or information is required for court proceedings, do not promise immunity from the hearing. Remember that you want this person to be on your client's side when in court, not smarting from trickery.

When a person agrees to make a statement take it there and then before they decide to change their mind. If too much time elapses they invariably go back on their word and prefer not to be involved.

CONFESSIONS

When approaching someone suspected of a crime or the guilty party in matrimonial proceedings, the object is to get a confession of guilt and if possible a voluntary statement to this effect.

You would first introduce yourself as a private investigator and then settle down comfortably for the interview. Name your client, explain the reason for your visit and—in some countries—administer what is known as the Short Caution. The wording of this is, 'You are not obliged to say anything, but anything you say may be given in evidence'. You may be asked to repeat this in court and it is necessary to know the wording by heart.

After cautioning the suspect (where this procedure applies), he will invariably make some reply and a note must be made of this AT THE TIME. A police officer would record this reply in his numerically paged notebook, but a private investigator usually carries the relevant file with him and he will probably make his notes at the time on a plain piece of foolscap. The sheet of paper would be prefixed with the time, date and place of the interview.

These three details, time, date and place, should be religiously adhered to in private investigation work. Everything should show them; statements, telephone messages and every notebook entry. Nothing should be excluded for these three facts have a very important bearing on all investigation matters.

Having recorded the verbatim reply of the suspect and presuming that it is an admission, caution him again and ask if he is prepared to make a written statement admitting the affair. In matrimonial cases the association with another party is generally admitted quite freely as most people in these circumstances want a divorce. In criminal cases the other party may well refuse to confess, but if the evidence is strong enough he will usually decide to make a statement.

A statement of confession is called either a Voluntary Statement or a Cautioned Statement and, as the former title suggests, it must be made quite voluntarily. No inducement should be offered to obtain a voluntary statement. Let the person write the statement himself if he so wishes. Although everyone must be given this choice, in practice they will invariably ask the investigator to write it for them.

Interrogation is an art in itself; some investigators can master it and others are quite hopeless. The more ruthless and stupid investigators who, thank goodness, are in a very small minority, often obtain their confessions by various dubious methods such as promising on behalf of their client that if stolen money is repaid the police will not be informed and no prosecution will take place. This may be a crime in itself committed by the investigator. Another type of inducement with adultery statements is to assure the co-respondent (the other man) that he will not be required to pay costs. This is quite misleading as only the court can decide this.

An investigator who conducts his business along these lines will be constantly accused of lying and eventually, even though nothing has been proved, he will gain a bad reputation and his business will suffer accordingly. If it were proved that he lied to the court on oath he would be charged with perjury.

One certainly has to have a certain dexterity of mind if one hopes to get results from interrogation, but this must not be confused with dishonesty. For instance, if the investigator is sure that a person has committed a crime but only one small piece of factual evidence is available, there would be harm in adopting a falsely confident attitude at the interview. Producing the one small piece of evidence at the right psychological moment can lead the suspect to acknowledge defeat. On the other hand, it would be dishonest to fabricate lies to obtain a confession. Remember, a suspect nearly always demands to know or see the evidence and any lying is usually a waste of time.

There are no two interviews alike and it will depend on the individual as to whether he is a good interrogator or not.

6
Cautions

(Applying only to countries where this form of warning is used)

As cautions are used in many countries where a suspect is being questioned, charged with an offence, or about to make a statement, it is felt advisable to touch at least generally upon this subject. It must be stressed that the cautions and information contained within the following paragraphs relate to English methods and other readers will have to adapt them to the structure of the law in their own country.

There are very specific rulings on this subject and they should be learned very thoroughly by anyone contemplating the occupation of private investigator. The admissibility of evidence in court oftens revolves around the very important question of 'Was the caution administered at the proper time?' or, 'Was the proper caution administered?' or the defence may try to contend that the caution was not administered at all.

If the case for the defence is rather weak without much chance of success, defence counsel may try his utmost to bring the credibility of the investigator's testimony into doubt. The favourite methods are to challenge the evidence as not being admissible since the defendant was:

1. Not cautioned at the time he made the verbal admission.
2. Cautioned too long after the admission, thereby making it inadmissible.
3. Not cautioned, and the investigator is merely including this in his evidence to make it admissible, i.e. he is lying.
4. Not asked to sign the caution at the beginning of the voluntary statement until the whole statement had been completed, thereby possibly making the statement inadmissible.

It can be seen therefore that it is essential to know when to caution and know by heart the wording of the caution.

The Short or Verbal Caution used in England (verify elsewhere)

'You are not obliged to say anything, but anything you say may be given in evidence.'

The written caution, which must precede all Voluntary or Cautioned Statements (N.B. Must be signed before the statement begins),

'I have been told by Mr .... that I am not obliged to make any statement unless I wish to do so and that anything I say will be taken down in writing and may be used in evidence.'
Signature of suspect ....

Now that the importance of the caution has been established, let us try to be a little more specific as to when and how it should be used. Remember that in law the use of the caution cannot be abused, so the rule should always be, IF IN DOUBT, CAUTION.

When an investigator is endeavouring to solve a crime, he will carry out numerous interviews to discover the guilty party. During these interviews which will usually be on a question and answer basis, there will obviously be no need to use the caution. However, immediately someone makes an incriminating remark, that person should be cautioned. If the caution is administered immediately after the remark it will still be admissible. On the other hand, if you have made up your mind that a person is guilty, caution AT ONCE before asking any questions or any further questions.

As many enquiries will relate to divorce proceedings where the caution is used several times, we will regard this subject in isolation. In most instances instructions are received from a law firm to the effect that the spouse of their client is committing adultery. He or she may be actually living with the other party, but if not they can often supply their name and address. This situation is a perfect example of the previous paragraph. You have made up your mind that they are guilty of adultery, therefore they should be cautioned at the very beginning of the interview, i.e. all replies would be after the caution.

When administering the verbal, short caution, try very hard

not to sound too officiously pompous. Some people find this most difficult to accomplish and often handicap themselves tremendously by frightening the interviewee into complete silence. They seem to find it necessary to stand upright, look very stern, raise their voice a few tones and repeat it like a parrot. Another very wrong way to cover this point is for the investigator to mention very casually something like, 'This might go to court you know'. This is utter stupidity as the caution must be in the EXACT WORDING as shown or it is unfair to the other party and means that the investigator commits perjury every time testimony is given in court.

There is no necessity for the caution to present the least problem, in fact it is probably easier to accomplish correctly than otherwise. Taken on its own the words may appear to be a little stilted, but remember that the exact words must be used. Therefore, to preserve a smooth continuity of speech which will not jar or frighten the listener, the caution could be put quite adequately in the following terms, 'You realize, of course, that you are not obliged to say anything, but anything you say may be given in evidence'. The five words preceding the caution make it far less awesome, but the suspect has been correctly warned.

In the same way, if an interview is being conducted and the interviewee says something incriminating, he can be cautioned quite sensibly by saying, 'Well, at this stage, in fairness to you, I must caution you that you are not obliged to say anything, but anything you say may be given in evidence'.

The caution can be adapted to the circumstances, but always remember that whatever is said must end with the exact wording of the short caution and any preliminary words should not affect or alter the meaning of the caution, but merely be an introduction to it.

To be a successful private investigator one must be fairly well aware of human nature. An exception to the foregoing might be the arrogant, loud-mouthed suspect, for whom an officious delivery of the caution would be more suitable, as it might deflate him long enough for the investigator to get the upper hand.

7
Statements, Reports and Identification

Many hours of a private investigator's life are spent in taking statements of one sort or another and he must train himself to become meticulously proficient. A statement is simply a written record of what a person can say about a certain happening. The object is, particularly in witness statements, to record a verbal picture of an event for the enlightenment of some person who was not there. When taking any type of statement it should always be borne in mind that it will have to be closely perused and the majority find their way into court. Therefore it is essential to develop a clear, neat style of handwriting so that the reader will not waste time trying to decipher your hieroglyphics. Most statements are taken in longhand, but it is always advisable to supply a typewritten copy to the client, together with the original, keeping another copy in the file. This copy statement must be carefully checked with the original and initialled to this effect.

Another point which must never be overlooked is the proper name of the witness. At first sight this may seem too obvious to mention but in practice numerous mistakes are made, either with a spelling error or overlooking a middle name. The latter often occurs because a person has an abhorrence to his middle name, therefore he has actually ceased to use it. One must be very precise in all matters appertaining to names. If a witness is asked for his name, or even if one goes so far as to say, 'Is that your full name?' he will invariably not mention his other name. To counteract any possibility of mistake ask the more direct question, 'Have you a middle name?' If it is pointed out that the witness has but never uses it, invariably gentle persuasion will reveal it. However unfortunate the name it must be included in the statement.

When taking a statement, the same rule always applies about putting the subject at ease and, within reason, giving him a free rein to air his views. Commandeer a good writing surface and then commence the statement, taking it stage by stage. In most cases it will be found that a good deal of concentration and perseverance is needed to keep the witness from straying off the point. Unless this is accomplished an enormous amount of time can be wasted.

Before approaching the witness, be aware of all the facts relating to the enquiry, particularly what your client is trying to establish, e.g. did he fall or was he pushed? However, a private investigator must never succumb to the temptation of manipulating a witness in such a manner that he alters his story, recounting and signing an untrue narrative that is more in keeping with the desires of the client. This is a most dangerous practice as it will mislead the client, and the witness will most assuredly give honest testimony in accordance with his pre-statement views once on oath in a courtroom. The case will be lost, the client put to unnecessary expense, and the incompetent investigator is going to look rather foolish. If the witness can only recount events which tend to be against the client, a statement should still be taken as this will help to reveal the strength of the opposition.

When taking a statement one should not lead the witness, but allow him to tell his own story in his own manner. Leading questions are only to be asked to clear up any ambiguity, e.g. if a witness says an occurrence happened on Monday, one may ask which Monday and at what time. However, in fact this rule is impractical. It is not suggested that one should induce a witness to sign an untrue statement, but if the witness does 'tell his own story in his own manner', say a foundry labourer who has seen a workmate caught up in an unguarded machine, his statement will be unnecessarily long and probably the relevant matter would still be missing. To some extent, therefore, one must assist the witness to shape his rather confused mass of facts into a more comprehensible form. With all statements the interviewee should agree to every sentence before it is committed to paper, and when completed, he should read it through very carefully and be given the opportunity of altering, adding or deleting any part of it.

Never alter words in a statement if they are wrong; cross them out and get the witness to initial the mistake at the side, or at the end of the line in the margin.

A witness should sign every sheet of the statement with his normal signature. Under the witness's signature at the end of the statement the investigator endorses in the following manner:

'The above statement was obtained by me at 9.30 p.m. (or between 8.45 p.m. and 9.30 p.m.) on .... day and date .... at .... full address ....
Signature.'

In the body of all statements, particularly voluntary or cautioned statements, try to record the actual words and phrases used by the witness, rather than your own grammar. In these circumstances slang is permissible, but do try to avoid an inarticulate jumble.

The ideal time to obtain a statement is immediately after the occurrence, whilst the facts are fresh. However, this is hardly ever the case, and where insurance claims are involved it may be a year or more before instructions are received.

An opinion as to where the blame lies can be included in a witness statement and although the opinion may not be allowed in the later court testimony it does sometimes help to assess the witness's true feelings. If annual holidays are near, include these dates in the statement so that any court hearing can be adjusted accordingly.

WITNESS STATEMENT—Example

PETER JOHN DAY states: I am 28 years of age, employed by William Dalby and Sons Ltd. of Rawside Mills, Greenside, London W.C.3, as a fitter. I reside at 65 King Street, London W.C.3 (Telephone No. XYZ 32481).

At about 10.30 p.m. on Tuesday, 14th November 19... I was walking along the nearside pavement in Town Street, London W.C.3, near to the junction with West Lane. I was walking towards Southgate. It was a dark night and there was some fog about. Visibility was down to about 25 yards. It was not raining at this time, but it had been raining and the road surface was wet. The tarmacadam road is in a good state of repair and well lit by sodium lamps. As far as I can remember they were all in working order on that night.

A Ford 12 cwt van (the registered number of which I now know to be ABC 123) passed me, going in the opposite direction. My memory of this is rather vague and I cannot remember the speed or position in the road. Almost immediately I heard a loud crash and upon looking round I saw that the Ford had collided head-on with an Austin motor car (Reg. No. DFG 456) which had been travelling in the opposite direction. This accident had happened at the bottom of West Lane. The Ford was on the wrong side of the road, pointing away from the city. The Austin was on the correct side of the road, near the crown, and pointing in the direction of the city. Extensive damage was caused to the front of both vehicles. I immediately ran to the scene and saw that the girl passenger in the Austin had streams of blood running down her face and I think that her head had gone through the windscreen, which was broken. I can also remember that the girl passenger in the Ford had injuries to her legs. Both drivers appeared unharmed. I then went to the nearest 'phone and notified the ambulance and police. These people were on the scene very quickly and both girls were taken to hospital. Neither of the vehicles was moved until after the police had arrived and taken measurements. At the time I did not give my opinion as to who was to blame, but I would say that the fault lies with the driver of the Ford van as he must have been driving on the wrong side of the road.

I did not smell any drink on either of the two drivers but this could be because I had been drinking myself that night, but only in moderation.

I am quite prepared to attend court to give evidence.

(usual signature) P. J. DAY

The above statement obtained by me at 6.40 p.m. on Tuesday, 18th April 19..., at 65 King Street, London W.C.3.

Signature

INDUSTRIAL ACCIDENTS

These cover such an enormous area it is impossible to even attempt any full explanations. They are usually involved with a workman having an accident during working hours, as a result of which he is suing employers or former employers for any loss sustained by the accident. This may be for a small or a very substantial amount, depending on the seriousness of his injuries. The employee accuses the employer of negligence contributing to his accident, and this is often denied. The employer is usually covered by insurance so in effect the fight is really between employee and the insurance company which holds the policy.

Unfortunately, this type of accident is very commonplace these days, the newspapers are full of them and they are usually caused either by negligence on the part of the employer or negligence by the employee, thereby being responsible for his own accident. If the employee agrees that the accident was due to his own negligence then the matter usually ends there, but if he sues the employer the allegation has to be investigated by both sides. The types of industrial accident vary considerably and often, realizing that the accident was due to their client's negligence, the insurance company will pay an agreed amount of damages rather than go into court. This is known as 'Settling out of Court'.

They might decide to fight the case and this is where the investigator begins his enquiries. He will receive detailed instructions from either the law firm acting for the employee or the insurance company. (He cannot work for both.) If he is working for the employer he will be trying to find witnesses in the factory who can say, and thus prove that the employee was to blame, and vice versa if he is on the other side. The employer and everyone else is usually in sympathy with the injured man and it would be very rare indeed to encounter any hindrance or ill-feeling during the course of enquiries. One might possibly take a set of photographs in order to be able to clarify certain points and a personal examination of the scene might also be made to discover the cause, or perhaps note that the fault causing the accident was now rectified. A detailed report of the investigator's findings may be submitted, but the real and most important evidence will come from independent witnesses who give statements proving that your side is in the right. Whatever the witnesses are going to say, whether for or against, take the statements as those will at least help to clarify the position. Where machinery is involved some difficulty may be encountered with all the technical names for the different parts, and after mentioning each strange name explain its purpose and position in normal language so that people who later read the statement will understand.

The following statement should give some general idea of what information is required. There is only one shown here but in practice there will be several witness statements to each accident.

PETER JOHNSON states: I am 27 years of age, a textile fitter and reside at ....

At about 9.30 a.m. on .... I was working with Mr .... at the premises of .... name and address .... At this time I was employed as a fitter by this firm, but I am now employed by .... name and address .... Tel. .... At this time we were completing the job of refitting the furnace at the end of the works. I was on top of the furnace, bolting a plate into position and Mr .... was on a plank supported by trestles at the side of the furnace, about four feet from the ground, helping me to fix on the plate. The whole furnace was very hot because it had been lit the previous day. We were given to understand that the furnace had been started in order to save time, so that the temperature could be built up to full pressure for the following day. It was very uncomfortable on top of the furnace and I could feel the heat through my boots. Alongside the furnace is a salt bath about 3 ft high, 2 ft wide and 8 ft in length. This holds a chemical mixture containing acid, which, when in full operation, is heated to a temperature 300 times that of boiling water. If even a splash of this liquid touches flesh or clothes, it immediately burns and is extremely dangerous. It had not reached maximum temperature when this accident occurred, but the temperature would be very high. There was no cover on the tank, although as a rule there is a combined wood and metal cover for part of the tank with the remainder of the opening covered by a wire mesh guard. This arrangement allows a large wheel to rotate through the tank. On this occasion neither of these covers was in place in the usual position and they had not been put back after the salt bath had been re-filled. As far as I can remember, Mr .... started to get down from the plank onto the ground, but in doing so he slipped and his right foot went into the uncovered tank of acid. He immediately pulled his foot out of the tank and we took him to the first-aid room where the ambulance was called and he was taken to hospital.

Without a doubt the fault of this accident lies in the fact that there was no cover over the tank at the time Mr .... fell. There were covers in existence but these were not being used. Immediately after the accident the covers were put on the tank and a few days later I was instructed to make metal guards to fasten on to the wire mesh so that the liquid would not even be able to splash through. Another thing that was to blame for the accident was that they should not have lit the furnace until we had completed the whole job as it made working conditions very awkward.

The man in charge of this operation was the chief engineer, Mr ...., but I am not aware of his address.

Usual signature

The foregoing statement was obtained by me at .... time, date and place ....
Signature

You will note that the main context of the statement is always contained in one long paragraph. This is particularly important in voluntary or cautioned statements and this practice must be strictly adhered to, the reason being that nothing can be added at some later stage, i.e. after it has been signed.

When dealing with industrial accident matters or any other type of enquiry, always be prepared to take a little extra trouble so that a situation can be clearly understood. Photographs can sometimes be of great assistance, as can sketches or drawings. It is not very difficult to draw a plan to scale, but if you are not particularly gifted in this sphere draw a sketch of the subject and insert the proper measurements. If the plan is not to scale the words 'Not to Scale' should be prominent. In this instance try to keep the dimensions in proportion so that it gives a fairly accurate impression.

Apart from industrial accident claims the private investigator will encounter many other forms of enquiry where the claimant is attempting to procure damages. Exactly the same principles apply; the investigator should try to honestly prove or disprove the allegations and there will usually be many statements involved.

If, when visiting the scene of the accident, there is nothing of significance to report, you would not submit an actual statement yourself but would mention any worthwhile features in the letter accompanying the file. In practice this is what usually happens, although on many occasions you will not be instructed to visit the scene but will obtain your statements at the witnesses' homes. However, if you discover something of real significance, which would tend to prove your client's claim, e.g. that the machine was still without a safety guard, then you would most definitely submit a full explanatory statement of your findings.

The first introductory paragraph of all your reports, whatever the enquiry, will always be the same and should read something like the following:

EDWARD COLLINS states: I am a private investigator, the principal of .... Detective Agency (or employed by .... Detective Agency) of .... address ....

If the enquiry was a long drawn out affair requiring interim reports, you would only use this wording on the first report and all subsequent ones would commence after EDWARD COLLINS further states:

After the introduction a new paragraph is begun with the usual time, date and place, recounting the events in sequence. Any direct speech should be shown as such, starting a new line with every question and every answer. Here is an example of how you might word your report:

Industrial Accident Report

At 9.45 a.m. on Monday .... I visited the premises of .... where I saw the manager, Mr .... I explained that I had been instructed by Messrs ...., solicitors acting on behalf of Mr .... to examine the scene of the accident. Mr .... took me into the ground floor machine room and pointed out the exact spot where Mr .... fell and broke his leg.

Upon examination I found that this area of the floor was spattered with oil and was extremely slippery. I pointed this out to Mr ....

He replied, 'I have told the cleaners about it but they don't seem to bother much in here'. The rest of the floor was in the same condition, making movement extremely precarious, particularly with the heavy machinery in such close proximity.

Signature
.... Detective Agency

In the above case, after you had seen the manager, you would obtain as many witness statements from as many other workpeople as possible. You would also ask the manager for a statement.

It is essential that the first part of your report—in any type of enquiry—should always identify very clearly the person who is being interviewed and also that they agree in direct speech to being that person. If a clear identification is not obtained the rest of the report can sometimes be invalid.

e.g. 'Are you John Peter Smith, the owner of motor car ABC 123?'
He replied, 'Yes'.

Always remember that a father and son might have the same first names so, although it is not necessary to show this in your statement, connect the subject of the enquiry to the person interviewed. Numerous mistakes are made, quite unnecessarily, over this subject of identification, causing a good deal of trouble to both investigator and client.

Equally, the same rules apply when a report is not involved. It might be the service of a writ or the verification of a trace, but it will only take a second to ask a further short question which will identify them undoubtedly with your enquiry.

If you can say from your own experience that you know a person the wording of your report would probably read:

'. . . where I saw Mr John Peter Smith, whom I know personally.'

PHOTOGRAPHS

Photographs, particularly in matrimonial cases, are a very common means of identification and the report would read:

'. . . where I saw Mr John Hobson, whom I identified by a photograph, which I had in my possession at the time, and which he endorsed. I now produce that photograph.'

The ideal photograph is one which is fairly recent and shows just the one person you wish to interview. The endorsement or signature should be written on the back.

In a matrimonial case, if not armed with a photograph, you would again carry out the identification by direct speech:

'Are you Mr John Peter Smith, the husband of Julia Smith who lives at ....?'
He replied, 'Yes'.

In this instance try to obtain a photograph from Mr Smith and get him to sign it on the back. Your actual report would not then need to mention the direct speech identification—although your notes made at the time would show it—and the report for court would read:

'. . . where I saw Mr John Peter Smith, whom I identify by the photograph, which I now produce, and which he endorsed.'

This method is just as efficient as the last, because in court the wife will identify the photograph and the signature as that of her husband and the signature will be the same as that on the confession statement and receipts. (i.e. Acknowledgement of Service.)

Introduction is a method which is often used in matrimonial cases in relation to the other party. In practice you are usually aware of the person's name and address, either by your own enquiries or through the knowledge of your client, but sometimes this information is not available when interviewing the guilty spouse, in which event he or she will either introduce you to the other party, or furnish their name and address. If the other party is present at the interview your report might read:

'. . . a woman was present and Mr Hobson introduced her to me as Mrs Alice Petty. I identify her by the photograph, which I now produce, and which she endorsed.'

As before, a photograph would be obtained at the time of interview. Although this identification is by no means as positive as that of the respondent, since the petitioner might not know the other party, it is accepted quite willingly by the court as the signature can be checked against the receipt. If the other party was not present at your interview with the guilty spouse, then you would see him as soon as possible and your report would show two distinct interviews.

HANDWRITING

The handwriting of a person can often have a bearing on identification and may be proved by:

1. The evidence of the writer himself.
2. A witness who actually saw the paper or signature written.
3. A witness who has a knowledge of the person's writing by having seen him write on other occasions.

4. A witness who has seen, in the ordinary course of business, documents presumably written or signed by the person.
5. Comparisons of the disputed writing with any writing proved to be genuine, made by witnesses acquainted with the handwriting or by skilled witnesses who are experts in handwriting.

The opinion of witness 3, 4 or 5, that the handwriting is genuine or not, is admissible evidence.

There are other methods of identification used by the police, e.g. identification parades, identification from a group of photographs; but these have no relevance to the private investigator.

NEGATIVE STATEMENTS

A negative statement is a statement taken from a person who denies knowledge of an alleged or suspected civil wrong, crime or offence. In some cases it can be extremely valuable, because if this person later gives evidence in court on behalf of the other party he can be challenged with the statement he made denying knowledge of the case. His evidence would thus be discredited. For example, if in a hotel case the assistant manager denied knowledge of seeing the suspected parties on the night in question, but from his demeanour it was suspected he was lying, it would be very useful to take a short negative statement. If he later appeared and wanted to say that he saw the man concerned alone on that particular night, his evidence would not be accepted.

Get the idea of this statement in the right perspective. A negative statement should only be taken on the very isolated occasions when you sense a vague possibility that a person may turn up later at the court hearing as a witness for the other side.

PETITIONS AND STATEMENTS

This is where clients are endeavouring to compile a petition to support their application for some licence, or other project. It could be for or against. The wording of the particular petition would be supplied by the client and would be contained at the top of each sheet of foolscap. The idea is to obtain hundreds of signatures and addresses in the surrounding area. These enquiries can be dealt with best between 6 p.m. and 10 p.m. when the workers have returned home, and several signatures can be obtained from each house. Only signatures which apply to the petition must be taken. For example, a fourteen-year-old signatory would have no bearing if the petition was for a new bar licence. Always ascertain roughly how many signatures are required and then work outwards from the central point until this target has been reached.

In most cases signatures are very easy to obtain, it being merely a matter of knocking on each door, briefly explaining the contents and asking for a signature and signatures from other members of the household. For convenience, it is best to keep the sheaves of the petition on a clip board. Bear in mind that these are not interviews; only a few seconds should be expended at each house as people are usually only too willing to sign. Do not waste time on the odd individual who wants to argue the finer points and is obviously not going to sign; leave him politely and move on to the next house.

It is not necessary to be an expert private investigator to obtain these signatures, in fact an eighteen-year-old girl probably has more appeal to the prospective signatory and this is one type of assignment where unskilled labour can be put to good use. Get as many people into the district as possible, allot each of them a particular area and arrange a later communal meeting point.

Apart from the signatures you will usually need a few good witnesses who are prepared to attend the court hearing. These should be chosen carefully from amongst the few people who are particularly intense in their support, but they should be completely independent of any association with the petitioners. Try to find the types who are of 'good witness material', i.e. reasonably fluent and intelligent.

Type of statement required:

JOHN PETER SMITH states: I am 38 years of age, a foreman joiner and reside with my wife and three children at ....

In the summer of .... I was asked to sign a petiton against the building of a new bar in .... Road, ... I refused to sign as I think that it is about time we had a few amenities on the estate and this would be a good start. It is a long way to the nearest bar, either up or down .... Road. If anyone from the estate goes into .... for a drink, they have to either catch the last bus back at 9.35 p.m., which means leaving a bar at 9.30 p.m., or walking back up the hill. This state of affairs is very bad for all the people on the estate, particularly the pensioners.

I have three children, the eldest is ten years old—and I am quite satisfied that the bar would in no way endanger their safety; in fact I think the site is in the ideal position.

I don't drink a great deal, but I am not against drinking and I feel sure that a bar would be a good social meeting place, making life more neighbourly on the estate.

I am quite prepared to attend court to give evidence.

Usual signature

The above statement obtained by me at .... time, date and place ....   Signed

It should be pointed out to all witnesses that there will be no monetary loss by their assisting the petitioner, in all cases they will be fully recompensed for travelling expenses and loss of earnings, but no other inducement should be offered.

You may also be asked to submit a report of your own about the area, detailing the distance from the proposed site to the nearest bar, for example.

STATEMENTS BY ILLITERATE PERSONS

It is very seldom that a completely illiterate person is encountered but when this does occur and the person is not even capable of signing his own name, a third party who is familiar with the illiterate should be present during the whole statement. They themselves would then have to make a short statement to this effect at the end of the caution—if applicable—and at the end of the statement. The illiterate would affix his mark, usually a cross, in the appropriate places.

The statement might take the following form:

I have been told by Mr Collins that I am not obliged to make any statement unless I wish to do so and that anything I say will be taken down in writing and may be used in evidence.

Affix mark X

EDWIN PATERSON states: I am 28 years of age, a mechanic and I reside at .... I am the brother of Mrs MARY SMITH and was present when Mr Collins read over the above caution to Mrs Smith and also explained its significance to her. She agreed to make a statement and affixed her cross before continuing.

Usual signature Edwin Paterson

MARY SMITH states: I am 33 years of age, a mill worker and reside at ....

I understand quite plainly what is being said to me, but I can neither read nor write.

(In the case of a foreign immigrant it must be shown more specifically that he understands the language, or an interpreter would be needed.)

e.g. I am a Pakistani immigrant and I came to this country two years and four months ago. Although I understand English and speak it well, I am afraid that I neither read nor write. I am content for Mr Abdul Singh to read the statement to me.

The statement is now continued in the normal manner and after it has been finished the third party should read it through to the illiterate, and if he agrees to it being the truth, it should be continued as follows:

I have had the above statement read over to me by Mr Paterson and I agree that it is true.

Affix mark X

EDWIN PATERSON further states: I have carefully read over the above statement to Mrs Smith and she has been given the opportunity of deleting, adding to, or altering any part of it. After agreeing that the statement was true she affixed her mark in my presence.

Usual signature Edwin Paterson

The above statement obtained by me at .... time, date and place ....

Edward Collins

This method is not always necessary in a normal witness statement—unless there is a possibility of them going back on their testimony on the grounds that they did not know what they were signing—but it MUST ALWAYS be used when taking a voluntary or cautioned statement from a suspect.

STATEMENTS THROUGH AN INTERPRETER

The use of amateur interpreters is not advocated in practice as they tend to *a)* be biased towards either the investigator or the witness, b) do not understand the proper duties of an interpreter, c) fail to make proper notes of the interview, and are regarded with much suspicion at the court hearing.

The best method is to contact the local police force where the Aliens' Department will have a full list of all their official interpreters. These are usually private citizens who held responsible positions in their own country. They should be persons of knowledge and ability in order to translate the words of the witness without any distortion of the facts. If there is any wilful distortion of the evidence at the later hearing they are committing perjury.

The fee will be in accordance with the local rates.

Difficulties can arise when an investigator has taken a voluntary statement from a person with the aid of an interpreter. If the interpreter is not called at the trial and the investigator simply narrates what the interpreter told him the accused had said, the evidence will be excluded as hearsay. The proper course is to call the interpreter who, with the help of his notes, will be able to give direct evidence of what the accused said, and the accused's statement will then be admissible. If, as sometimes happens, the interpreter is unable to remember what took place, and if he did not take notes at the time, he can only swear that he made a true translation. Bearing this in mind, always make sure that the interpreter is also making independent notes of the interview.

A statement through an interpreter should be along similar lines to the following:

> I have been told by Mr Collins that I am not obliged to make any statement unless I wish to do so and that anything I say will be taken down in writing and may be used in evidence. The caution has been translated and explained to me by the interpreter Mr Steiner and I understand its implication.
>
> Kurt Schmidt

FRITZ STEINER states: I am a naturalized .... subject and have been in this country for fifteen years. My country of origin was .... where I was a fully qualified solicitor. I am now self-employed as an interpreter and am on the list of official interpreters for the .... City Police. I have translated and explained the above caution to Mr Schmidt. He agrees to make a statement and has signed the caution before continuing.

Fritz Steiner

KURT SCHMIDT states: I am 31 years of age, a chef, and reside at .... I am a .... citizen and have only been in this country for the past five months. I neither speak, read nor write the English language.

The statement should now be continued in the normal manner, going over each sentence very clearly so that any ambiguities can be clarified. The man should tell his story in his own language and the interpreter should translate a true version into English. When the statement is completed the interpreter must read it through, giving the person a chance to alter it if he so wishes. When he agrees that it is correct the following words should be written.

I have had the above statement read over to me in my own language and I confirm that it is true.

Kurt Schmidt

FRITZ STEINER further states: To the best of my ability, I have truly translated Mr Schmidt's words into the .... language as set forth in the foregoing statement. I have read the statement over to him in his own language and have given him the opportunity of deleting, adding to or altering any part of it. He agrees that it is a true version of his narrative and as such signed it in my presence and in the presence of Mr Collins.

Fritz Steiner

The above statement obtained at .... time, date and place.

Edward Collins

The interpreter should then submit a report—probably dictated and typed immediately at your office—outlining the events leading up to the taking of the statement; that he accompanied you, the identification was made by direct speech or by photograph, the questions asked, etc. The investigator also submits a report containing exactly the same details, mentioning that everything he said was translated. Thus if both the interpreter and the investigator each adhered faithfully to the practice of making their notes actually at the time of interview, then the text of both reports would be more or less identical.

CRIME STATEMENTS AND REPORTS

It will sometimes be necessary to take witness statements from someone who can impart information about the committing of a crime. These will be taken in the same manner as mentioned earlier in this chapter. The only point to make a special note of is that they must reveal, if possible, how the crime was executed, as it is these facts which classify the crime.

Apart from this, all other statements in relation to confessing crime will be voluntary or cautioned statements. When taking them it is essential to know what specific crime has been committed in order to include all the ingredients required by law to prove that particular offence. This does not mean that words should be put into the suspect's mouth, on the contrary, this must never be attempted. However, it is perfectly correct to clear up any ambiguities and if during the course of a confession statement a man admitted taking money or goods, it would be quite in order to ask him exactly how the theft was carried out.

In both criminal and matrimonial investigations, the admissibility in evidence of a voluntary or cautioned statement depends largely upon the manner in which it was obtained. There should not be any inducements or threats of any kind, and the person making the voluntary statement should be of sound mind.

In voluntary statements where a confession is obtained, the guilty party invariably offers to return the goods or repay the stolen money. However, this does not mean that he will necessarily avoid prosecution and this inducement should not be offered to him.

Example of Typical Confession Statement

I have been told by Mr Collins that I am not obliged to make any statement unless I wish to do so and that anything I say will be taken down in writing and may be used in evidence.

Jack Haley

JACK HALEY states: I am 37 years of age, married and live with my wife and two children at .... I was employed by JOHNSON HARDWARE LIMITED, of .... from .... to .... as the manager. My first assistant at the shop was Mrs SHEILA JONES. We became very friendly and used to go out together. When I left the shop in .... date .... Sheila became manageress and I worked for .... of .... In .... date .... I decided that I would like to start up my own business and began purchasing small quantities of goods from the JOHNSON HARDWARE shop. The quantities soon became much larger and I only paid for a small portion of the goods I took out of the shop. I was still working for .... up to .... date .... and during this period I was building up capital to start in business on my own. I know that I got a considerable amount of goods from the shop which I did not pay for and which I honestly admit even at the time of delivery had no intention of paying for. Mrs Jones was well aware that I was doing this but, although she was a party to it, she did not benefit in any way. From .... to the end of .... I was ill and didn't work, but on .... date .... I started up in business on my own account at .... and the business goes under the name of HALEY'S HARDWARE STORE. This is a retail hardware shop and I would say that it was started mainly by money which I obtained by selling the goods I had wrongfully obtained from the JOHNSON HARDWARE shop. The amount of money or value I wrongfully obtained from the shop would be about £ .... (words) .... and I realize now that I have been an absolute fool. If I am given the opportunity I will pay it all back in the shortest possible time, even though this may mean severe hardship for myself and family.

I have read the above statement and it is true.

Jack Haley

The above statement obtained at .... time, date and place ....

Edward Collins

N.B. The foregoing statement will take up more than one piece of foolscap. When this happens the person making the statement should sign the first sheet and the caution would then be written out again in full on the second sheet. The second caution should be signed and the statement continued thus:

JACK HALEY further states:

It is hoped that the foregoing chapter will give the investigator enough guidance to be able to formulate statements and reports applicable to any situation which might arise. It is obviously impossible to attempt a full coverage of every type of investigation, but basically all investigations follow the same pattern and the identical rules apply.

The investigator's report is always typewritten on plain, foolscap paper, accompanied by a letter on his firm's notepaper.

Most statements are taken in longhand and remember with cautioned statements that the caution should be written out in the suspect's presence and signed BEFORE continuing with the actual narrative.

8
Matrimonial Enquiries—Adultery

BURDEN OF PROOF (Adultery)

It is not necessary to prove the direct fact, it would be a rare occurrence to surprise the parties actually in the act of adultery, *and such evidence would probably be disbelieved.* The fact is inferred from the circumstances. The two main facts to prove are OPPORTUNITY and INCLINATION.

EVIDENCE OF PAID DETECTIVE

As the court frequently acts on the uncontradicted evidence of a reliable investigator as it is often the only evidence available, great care must be taken.

We now come to the practical aspects of the subject, as they will apply to the private detective.

TAKING INSTRUCTIONS

These will come from either law firms or private clients and it is imperative that the investigator should be in possession of all the facts from the very outset of the enquiry. It is up to the investigator to make sure that his instructions are complete enough to enable him to carry out his duties effectively.

The instructions from solicitors will seldom present any problems, but you may have to ask an odd question to reveal some relevant point. They will either send a fully detailed letter about a matrimonial enquiry, ask you to call at their office, or instruct over the telephone.

With private clients the question of fees must be carefully

considered and discussed on every occasion, otherwise you may incur substantial costs which the client is either unwilling or unable to pay. If they have very limited means and yet seem to have genuine grounds for suspicion, you can accept small weekly instalments until a reasonable deposit has accumulated. At this stage the investigation would commence.

Obtaining the proper details at the initial interview is more difficult with a private client. Treat them gently at all times, remembering that they are revealing very private, personal and sometimes heartbreaking details to a complete stranger. This will probably be the first time in their lives that they have been confronted with a private investigator and unless your attitude is appropriately sympathetic their full cooperation will not be forthcoming.

DETAILS REQUIRED

1. Client—full name and address.
2. Petitioner—full name and address (may also be a client).
3. Respondent—full name and address.
4. Co-respondent/Woman Named—if known, full name and address.
5. Photograph of respondent (also co-respondent if possible).
6. Place and date of marriage.
7. Names and birth dates of all children of marriage.
8. Which schools they attend.
9. Who has custody—legal custody or otherwise?
10. Is adultery admitted?
11. Are parties prepared to give statements?
12. Brief history and other relevant details, e.g. their suspicions, etc.
13. Observations required?
14. What is the initial fee to which you must work?

THE FILE

After obtaining all the above details the next step is to begin a file. This would most probably be of the foolscap variety. All papers appertaining to the enquiry would from then onwards be fixed onto the paper fastener in the file, with strict adherence to date-order. Further reports and telephone messages will then be added as the enquiry advances.

In all matrimonial statements made by the guilty parties under caution and relating to adultery, certain basic essentials must be proved to the satisfaction of the court before a decree can be granted. Because of this it is necessary, in most cases, to obtain the information covering these essentials by question and answer. However, write the statement in the exact form of the replies and let the parties tell the general history of the marriage in their own words, remembering that all the points must be answered, otherwise the statement is valueless. Have them agree each sentence before writing it down and, as with all voluntary or cautioned statements, let them read it through at the end, giving them an opportunity to add, alter or delete any part of it.

To eliminate the possibility of overlooking one of these points, it is a very good idea to make a condensed list of them in order of precedence, carrying this in your wallet at all times. When taking a statement use the list as a constant reminder of the exact details required.

ITEMS TO BE INCLUDED OR PROVED IN EVERY ADULTERY STATEMENT

Respondent's Statement
1. The caution.
2. General (marriage, children and schools).
3. The first time and place of adultery, and subsequent adultery. Name of co-respondent or woman named.
4. History of association and adultery to date—any future intentions? (marriage, etc.).
5. Mr X knew that I was a married woman from the beginning of our association—(this must be included, or words of the same meaning, in every statement by a woman respondent and every co-respondent. If not the petitioner will not be able to claim costs from the co-respondent).
6. I have read the above statement and it is true.
7. Examine bedroom and also children's bedrooms to satisfy court that the couple are living together and the children are well cared for.

Co-respondent's Statement (if present at above statement)
(or Woman Named)
1. Caution—signed.
2. I was present when Mrs X made and signed the above statement and I confirm that it is true.

3. I knew that she was a married woman from the beginning of our association.

N.B. In spite of the above statement being allowed in some courts, it might very well not be regarded as admissible in others—or at least it may create problems. With this in mind it is much better to take another full statement from the other party.

Co-respondent's Statement (if not present at the interview) (or Woman Named)

In this case a full statement must definitely be taken. The text of all co-respondent's statements must contain a passage which will inform the court that he knew the woman was married at the very beginning of their association. This enables the petitioner to ask for costs against the co-respondent. However, this is not necessary in a woman named statement, as costs are generally paid by the male respondent. There are very isolated exceptions to this rule, but in general these can be disregarded for any exception would be pointed out by your instructing solicitor.

OBTAINING THE CONFESSION STATEMENTS

From couple living together as man and wife

These are the easiest and most straightforward statements to obtain as the couple are 'living in sin' and usually want this state of affairs to end as quickly as possible.

It will be necessary to have the file so that details of marriage and date of parting can be easily referred to, photographs and plain foolscap. One piece of foolscap will be used by the investigator for all his notes, which he can later refer to in court. Two other pieces of foolscap will be needed for the confession statements. After obtaining the statements the investigator must examine the bedroom for conclusive proof that the couple are genuinely living together as man and wife.

The first statement is usually obtained from the respondent.

Respondent

I have been told by Mr Collins that I am not obliged to make any statement unless I wish to do so and that anything I say will be taken down in writing and may be used in evidence.

Usual signature

JOHN SMITH states: I am the husband of VERA SMITH. We were married on the .... at .... Church, ... town .... We had one child, Graham, born .... who lives with my wife. It is true that I have committed adultery with Mrs WINIFRED JACKSON. We first met in August .... and started to go out together. The first time that we committed adultery was when my wife was away on holiday at .... place .... This was during the beginning of August .... and it took place at my home .... address .... We continued to go out together and to commit adultery until my wife discovered our association and as a result she left me. This was on the .... of February, 19... and Winifred commenced to live with me at .... address .... on the same day. We are still living together at this address as man and wife and intend continuing to do so. As a result of our association together Winifred is now having a baby, which is due to be born on the 15th January, 19... I acknowledge that I am the father of this child. Winifred is married, but if she obtains her freedom and if this divorce is granted we shall then get married.

I have read the above statement and it is true.

Usual signature

The above statement obtained at .... time, date and place.

Signed

Woman Named

I have been told by Mr Collins that I am not obliged to make any statement unless I wish to do so and that anything I say will be taken down in writing and may be used in evidence.

Usual signature

WINIFRED JACKSON states: I was present when Mr JOHN SMITH made the statement admitting adultery with me and I confirm that it is true. We first met in August .... and committed adultery at the beginning of the same month at John's home .... We continued to go out together and to commit adultery until the .... of February ...., when we started to live together at this address and intend to continue in that state. If this divorce is granted and if I could obtain my freedom we would then get married.

I have read the above statement and it is true.

Usual signature

The above statement obtained at .... time, date and place.

Signed

N.B.: In countries where divorce is prohibited, leave out all reference to divorce and intention to get married.

INVESTIGATOR'S REPORT (typewritten and compiled by reference to notes made at the time of interview)

EDWARD COLLINS states: I am a private investigator and the principal of .... Detective Agency.

At 8.30 p.m. on .... full date .... I went to the house .... full address .... when I saw Mr JOHN SMITH. I identify him by the photograph, now produced, which he endorsed.

A woman was present and he introduced her to me as Mrs WINIFRED JACKSON.

I introduced myself, cautioned them and said, 'I have been instructed to see you with regard to your association together. I understand that you are living here as man and wife.'

Mr Smith replied, 'We are not going to deny it.'

Mrs Jackson replied, 'Yes, in fact I'm having a baby in January.'

I then asked them if they were prepared to make written statements admitting their adulterous association together and pointed out that these would be used in evidence in civil proceedings.

I again cautioned them and they agreed to do so.

I then obtained the statements, now produced, which they read over and signed in my presence and in the presence of each other.

I examined the bedroom and found that it was furnished with a double bed, double wardrobe and dressing table. There were articles of male and female clothing in the room and I was quite satisfied that they were living together as man and wife.

      Signature

      .... *Detective Agency*

N.B. If children of the marriage were present you would then mention having seen them and that they appeared to be quite happy and well cared for—providing they were. You would also examine the children's sleeping quarters to satisfy the court that the facilities were adequate.

NOTES MADE AT THE TIME OF INTERVIEW

The notes can be as brief as the investigator's memory allows, but remember that you deal with a tremendous amount of cases and you are only allowed to refresh your memory in court from notes which were actually made at the time of the interview. Do not leave blank lines. Initial the notes as soon as completed.

It is both inconvenient and inconsequential for the private investigator to keep a numerically paged notebook for his notes of interviews and replies. Firstly, he would probably have to stagger into court with about ten notebooks, each one referring to a separate case, i.e. divorce hearings do not come up immediately, like police matters. Secondly and probably most important, although seldom considered, is the very glaring fact that a constable's notebook and entries are checked and initialled daily by a superior officer, thereby ensuring the authenticity of the entries. The fact that a private investigator worked with a numerical notebook would not prove the slightest authenticity of the entries, as the main ingredient to ensure this, the daily supervision and initialling of a superior officer against each item, is missing.

STATEMENTS OBTAINED AT THE CONCLUSION OF OBSERVATIONS

Providing the parties are prepared to give statements, they would take the same form as usual. The only difference would be in a slight alteration of the investigator's direct speech on his first approach. After the identification and introductions had been established he would caution them and say, 'Observations have been kept on this house over the past two weeks and from these observations I have reason to believe that you have committed adultery together.'

If the parties agree, then you take the statements in the normal manner and only the few words of direct speech in your report show any deviation from the usual practice. The reports of observations would be kept on the file, but in most instances they would not be referred to and the guilt of the parties would be adequately proved by the confession statements.

REPORTS OF OBSERVATIONS

These are extremely important and must be compiled with an almost fanatical attention to minute detail, showing an exact record of:

1. Time and date observations commence.
2. When subject appears—mode of identification, e.g. photograph, personal description and type of car etc., or all three.
3. Place under observation or route taken by subject.
4. Exact time of all events to be recorded—if possible as they happen or as soon as possible afterwards.
5. Record time and place of meeting other party, plus full description of other party—including dress.
6. Record exact times of where they go and what they do. (Type of drink, dancing, holding hands, sitting on their own in a corner, etc.).
7. Observe until they part and then follow the unknown party home. Note exact address and check next day in the Electoral Register, or if apparently under 18 years, get the surname and make some very discreet enquiries in the vicinity in order to obtain an identification.
8. Keep up the observations until you consider enough incriminating evidence has been established.
9. If your client considers the evidence to be sufficient or the right psychological moment has arrived, then interview and if possible obtain statements.

All notes of observations should be made in longhand and each incident will start with the exact time. It will be these notes, made at the time, which will later be referred to in court. From these notes you will compile your typewritten report and, for convenience and easy reference, it is better to use separate sheets of paper for each period of observation, initialling or signing them on completion.

Remember never to leave the scene directly the lights go out, always wait about half an hour to prove beyond doubt that they were in the darkened house for a reasonable period of time.

Observations are sometimes only on a house, to prove that two people are living together as man and wife, or on a couple committing adultery in a parked car; but basically the investigator's job is the same on all occasions—to note the exact time of everything which occurs and to make a full note of each detail, however small, which tends to prove first the friendliness and familiarity; second the adultery.

OBSERVATIONS

This is another art which will have to be acquired. One of the main and rather obvious points is to be as inconspicuous as possible by wearing appropriately anonymous clothes, etc.

The following miscellany of hints will be useful in all branches of investigation work where surveillance is required.

1. The ideal position is one where you have an excellent view of the subject but where he cannot see you.
2. Never make any exaggerated avoidance movements, these will create suspicion.
3. When following on foot, keep just in sight unless in a busy street or in a position where the subject could easily disappear, such as near alleyways, junctions or down subways.
4. When following by car in a city, it is essential that a fairly close distance is kept, otherwise the other vehicle may turn out of sight while you are held up at traffic lights, etc. When more open country is reached then it is wise to drop back, to become less conspicuous on empty roads. A good rule in these circumstances is to keep one or two cars between you and the subject.

    Be very much on the alert for quick turns, stops or slowing down as these are the main danger periods and if they are not dealt with smoothly and naturally the subject could easily become suspicious. These manoeuvres can be practised easily without causing embarrassment or danger to anyone, if executed with due care.

    If it is possible to use different cars on different occasions do so.

    Unless by previous experience you are aware of a set route, never try to be too clever in anticipating the subject's destination. It is easy to lose them in this way.

    If the enquiry is important then two cars could be used to good advantage, providing the various changeovers take place smoothly. The ideal situation, of course, would be for the cars to be in radio contact.

    Make sure that there is sufficient petrol in the tank!
5. Invest in a good pair of binoculars.
6. If you have to work in a factory during an investigation, make sure that your appearance is not different to the other workers. Keep some old clothes and an old pair of overalls for this purpose.
7. Have a pair of good quiet shoes so that you can move about silently.

8. If stationary observations are necessary, do not sit obviously outside a house or other place in a car with the windows steamed up. The ideal vehicle for this—particularly in the daytime—is a small van with an old blanket draped from the roof to the floor, immediately behind the driver and passenger seats; the rear windows whitewashed lightly on the inside, enabling the watcher to see out, but nobody can see in. The watcher gets in the back of the van, an associate then drives it to the required position, locks it up and returns to drive it away at a pre-arranged time. Apart from the watcher being noisy or puffing smoke out of the air vents, there is little possibility of him ever being discovered.
9. Always look for and be prepared to grasp at any opportunity which arises. If stationary observations are needed have a swift look round the immediate viewing area for a room to let, a hotel, a derelict building or some other vantage point. These are usually far better and much less suspicious than being on foot or in a car or van.
10. Do not think that because the actual subject of your observations has not seen you that it is alright for you to be seen by other persons. Although you would not be discovered immediately, it will probably get back to your subject, making future observations utterly impossible.
11. Remember that at night any noise or light is easily discernible.
12. If the surveillance is on foot and at night, park the car well out of the way so that it will not draw unnecessary attention when driving off.
13. If you have to keep an all night vigil in a factory or site office, get well wrapped up in warm clothing and take some food and drink along.
14. Keep a constant watch on the subject at all times. If you are not prepared to do this there is no point in even starting the surveillance. Remember always that observations require 100 per cent concentration, nothing less will do.
15. Funds being available, take advantage of all the new modern innovations which appear on the market.
16. It is imperative to be a good driver. High speeds must sometimes be maintained, therefore you should endeavour to attain the competence of the advanced driver. Several good books have been written on this subject, and there will usually be local advance driving courses.
17. During evening observations you are less conspicuous if accompanied by a companion, but this is not by any means imperative.
18. As there are usually many slack periods make comprehensive

notes. This helps later in court and it also enables you to dictate the events in the form of a report very quickly.
19. Unless absolutely essential, never get into converation with the subject. When revealing yourself at a subsequent interview, they will accept the observations as part of your occupation, but an earlier conversation will be taken as a personal affront since they will feel that they have been unfairly tricked. These circumstances may result in an abortive interview.
20. Finally, remember always that you have no police powers with regard to speed limits, or anything else. Do not abuse the individual's right to privacy and be aware of the Law of Trespass.

VERBAL CONFESSIONS

There are numerous instances when a verbal confession is made, not only in relation to matrimonial investigations. Verbal confessions could be described as rather 'thin evidence' but nevertheless they can usually be put to good use, particularly if there is other corroborating evidence to back them up. Obviously these confessions must have been made under caution, or the caution administered immediately afterwards, otherwise they would not be admissible in evidence. A careful note should be made immediately of the actual words which are orally declared.

If a respondent or suspect is approached and a statement obtained in the normal manner, but upon taxing the other party or accessory they refuse to commit anything to writing, at the same time agreeing that the statement is true; this is a good Verbal Confession and their words of agreement should be instantly recorded. In the case of a co-respondent, although the point will have been brought out in the respondent's statement nevertheless to clarify the position beyond doubt, ask 'Did you realize that Mrs .... was a married woman from the beginning of your association with her?' The reply may be, for example, 'Oh, yes, I can't deny that.'

A series of good observations might be on file but when the parties are challenged with the evidence they refuse to make statements, but agree verbally that they have committed adultery together. Sometimes one party agrees at one interview but withdraws the verbal confession at the next, probably after consulting the co-respondent or a solicitor. One party might admit the adultery quite freely, but the other adamantly denies it. Record, under caution, and verbatim, both the confessions and denials, leaving it up to your clients to decide the strength of the case.

If the observations are good enough it is really immaterial whether the parties admit or deny the allegations, although it is preferable and much more simple if statements are made.

Verbal confessions, which are not supported by good corroborating evidence, will not generally be considered positive enough to take into court. However, there may be corroborating evidence of which you are not aware, e.g. a statement made by another witness, a birth certificate of an illegitimate child, or an incriminating letter. Therefore, when a verbal confession has been made the investigator must always submit a full report.

Having said all this, it must be made evidently clear to the private investigator that usually verbal confessions are not a very satisfactory form of evidence and at best their highest value could only be described as 'better than nothing'.

WHY DO PEOPLE MAKE CONFESSION STATEMENTS?

The reason for this is not, as some people would have us believe, because of the unfair methods of the investigator or the police detective. It is simply because, knowing or being informed of all the facts, they decide completely of their own volition that under the circumstances—be they civil or criminal —their own best interests will be served by making a statement. Certainly in most of the cases that the private investigator deals with, this is quite true; in fact in some instances it would be downright folly for the party not to make a voluntary statement.

In the following text you will be able to appreciate more clearly exactly how the truth of this statement is borne out.

DIVORCE STATEMENTS

Couple living together as man and wife

These people obviously have a good deal of affection for each other and hope to get married in the future. Even though both might be married and one spouse refuses to institute proceedings at this stage, they will probably change their minds later. It is also morally right that the innocent spouse should be able to obtain his or her freedom. In the event of them both having a reasonable hope of future freedom, they would then be utterly foolish not to make statements.

Not living together but committing adultery regularly

These people may, or may not, have an affection for each other. If they have and would like to get married then they will be only too pleased to make statements. If they have no intention of getting married they usually feel that even under these circumstances it is better to give statements, rather than defend an expensive divorce action.

In reaching this decision they consider:

1. The substantially increased cost of a defended action. The cost of an undefended petition is almost insignificant compared to a large defended case.
2. The extensive and often unsavoury character of the publicity.
3. If the case is undefended, the 'other woman's' name may not appear in the newspapers.
4. The waste of time and the embarrassment of appearing in court. (In countries where the guilty parties do not appear in undefended actions.)
5. The additional embarrassment to the person with whom adultery was committed.
6. The possible ruination of their social life.
7. If discovered, the possibility of the affair breaking up the 'other party's' marriage.
8. An adverse effect on their business or employment.
9. And last, but by no means least, the most undeniable feature of all. That they are aware of their guilt and know that the petitioner is both legally and morally right in taking the necessary action to end the marriage.

After considering these points it becomes a little more clear why people willingly make statements admitting a matrimonial offence. There is no doubt that in the majority of cases a full and frank disclosure is by far the best course.

CRIMINAL STATEMENTS

With a few exceptions, the private investigator seldom deals with the half illiterate type of hardened criminal encountered daily by the police. His assignments usually involve, for want of a better word, the more 'respectable' type of citizen, such as company secretaries, club treasurers, works managers, salesmen, shop managers and manageresses, etc.

Whenever this class of people is encountered, the investigator has a tremendous psychological advantage over the suspect. When confronted with the allegations of dishonesty they invariably become quite emotionally distressed and can only think of the overwhelming disgrace which they have brought upon themselves, and their families.

In making a statement these people consider:

1. The evidence, usually of a documentary nature in the majority of cases, is quite damning and wholly unanswerable.
2. That if they co-operate and tell the whole truth the court may be inclined to take a lenient view.
3. That there will be little or no publicity with a plea of guilty.
4. The thought of their workmates and immediate superiors being brought into the matter as witnesses, if no confession.
5. The very forlorn hope that if they co-operate and offer to repay the stolen monies, their employers might not prosecute.
6. Upon discovery, their conscience is working overtime and a confession tends to ease the strain a little. It has been said that 'confession is good for the soul'.
7. That a confession statement will both simplify and end the investigation, thereby cancelling out any further enquiries or expense for their wronged employers.
8. That dealing with a private investigator employed by their own firm is preferable to the police, even though they may be called in later.

FEES

One of the very first things a new private investigator should do is to find out what fees are already being charged in his particular area, and be guided by these. If an account appears to be exorbitant, have a personal word about it with your client, explaining the circumstances. If the account is genuine and the work justified, there should be no problem.

9
Criminal Investigations

The main single attribute needed to carry out this work is simply common sense. A good detective is not endowed with any supernatural powers, but perhaps his ability to perceive should be cultivated to the highest possible degree.

It is frequently said that experience is the main qualification of the detective, but this is a very old-fashioned way of thinking and is simply not true. The young, knowledgeable and enthusiastic investigator, possessing a high proportion of common sense, will invariably leave the stolid, experienced detective at the starting post. The older detectives and private investigators tend to lose their earlier enthusiasm, making them not inefficient but more suitable for a less demanding way of life, perhaps in an administrative capacity. These comments are not meant disparagingly, but there is no denying that when a man reaches late middle age he must prefer his fireside and bed, rather than staying up all night waiting for some thief to appear. There may be exceptions to this rule, but very few.

The best detective is the single-minded, dedicated young man of cheerful disposition who, when necessary, is prepared to work 'twenty-five' hours a day.

Criminal investigation by the private detective is not particularly exciting in the accepted sense of the word, neither is 99.9 per cent of police detection. There are seldom guns or knives, but it certainly does possess a certain fascination and has a different kind of excitement which can seldom be surpassed in this day and age by many other occupations. Many assignments will be rather mundane, but he will frequently be called upon with regard to some really interesting matter requiring all his ingenuity. It is with these assignments that he will discover the exciting fascination of fitting together the jumbled pieces of evidence which finally solve the case and allow the investigator to emerge triumphant, in a radiant glow of well-earned satisfaction. These few cases per year act as the perfect shield to boredom.

When investigating any case you should always be in the right state of mind. So many detectives lose the battle before leaving the office. Recognize a difficult case but never start with a defeatist attitude. Sternly subdue any thoughts of failure, and attack the problem with a completely open mind and an optimistic conviction of success. Always stay with this principle and you will find that over the years many difficult assignments will be brought to successful fruition.

Be thorough and, particularly when interviewing, be prepared for the unexpected. It often happens that during the course of your investigation a very valuable piece of information will come from a most unexpected source, but if you are not always alive to this possibility the clue will be missed. A sudden start or an embarrassed blush can make it obvious that the interviewee knows more about the subject than they admit. This is a valuable piece of information in itself, as it usually reveals other interesting avenues of enquiry. Generally it is not grand discoveries which solve criminal investigations, but small pieces of information which, when collected and pieced together, point in the direction of one culprit.

In many cases the investigator will more or less know from the outset who is the guilty party. The client is well aware of this, but requires proof before taking any further action. Never barge in and interview, hoping for an easy confession, as it may end with the investigator answering a slander charge. As a last desperate resort this may sometimes be justified, but you will have to be very wary in the wording of your interview, particularly if other witnesses are present. Much better to be armed with some evidence of guilt, thereby justifying your action.

TAKING INSTRUCTIONS

These are general requirements and will need to be adapted to fit the particular offence reported. Great attention should be paid to the finer details as these often reveal a wealth of useful information. If your client is definitely going to prosecute and there appears to be a reasonable chance of success, then the instructions could be taken in the form of a statement. This would save time at a later date and could be handed over to the police to facilitate their prosecution. Instil confidence in the client with a positive attitude to his problem, get his views, but be firmly in control of the interview and make sure that all your questions are answered.

Never allow a client to carry you along with his own ideas of how the enquiry should be conducted. They are usually intelligent people of substance who can often offer some valuable hints about their own particular problem. However, any schemes suggested should be very carefully considered before embarking on a course of action which may well alert the opposition and ruin your chances of gaining the important advantage of surprise. In practice it will be found that most of these ideas revolve around one scrap of vague information which the client wrongly believes to be valuable evidence. The aim should be to collect carefully all the available evidence, thus strengthening your position for the final interview. There are exceptions, but in most cases interviewing the suspect will be the last step, not the first.

There are certain types of criminal enquiry which are common to all detective agencies, appearing with constant regularity. These will be outlined in the following pages.

RETAIL SHOP MANAGERS—*Dishonesty*

A dishonest manager or manageress of a retail store is probably the most common of all criminal investigations encountered. This type of dishonesty is usually discovered at the annual stocktaking, when the owners are not satisfied that the deficiency can be written off to customers' pilfering or excessive but genuine trade discounts.

Once the deficiency is certain, investigations can proceed.

The first and most obvious step is to look for documentary proof at the actual premises. This must be done secretly, at a time when nobody will accidentally see what is happening. Of course, if you are in possession of a till roll or receipt book which does not tally with the shop returns, then you already have nominal proof of guilt. However, a few isolated acts of dishonesty are easily countered by an explanation of genuine mistake, and this will probably be accepted by the court. In the first instance, this is often the excuse when you have irrefutable evidence!

In exceptional cases of stock deficiency the thieves may have simply driven it away in a vehicle, in which case there would be no incriminating documents to find. However, usually the fraud is manipulated over the shop counter and once suspected, guilt can be proved in many ways.

Some of the more common points to look for are:

1. An unofficial second receipt book.
2. Entries in the official receipt book which do not correspond with the till roll. A common practice is to record say £5·00 as 50p. This satisfies the customer and if they make any comment it can be laughed off as a mistake.
3. An unusual amount of 'No Sale' marks on a till roll, although not evidence, is highly suspicious.
4. Check all numerical books for missing pages.
5. Check all delivery notes against the till roll, where cash has been paid.
6. Take special note of wholesale customers and make sure that you obtain names and addresses. If there is any conspiracy with the customers it is often among the regular tradesmen.
7. The floor and waste baskets often reveal wonderful evidence. For instance a customer's abandoned receipt or the crumpled counterfoil of a receipt book, etc. Check these items against the till roll and returns.
8. Make a special note of names where addresses are also shown, plus the quantities and cash sale record. These people might then be discreetly interviewed about their purchases.
9. Study the particular system of recording sales, noting them down step by step, and look for possible loopholes.

TEST PURCHASES

Test purchases might be the next step in the enquiry if there is not enough evidence to justify an interview, and these can be carried out with two or three people.

They must be worked out carefully with a responsible member of the company, and you will need to know the exact price of a few items which are within easy reach of the counter and are asked for daily. All the people taking part in this exercise must know, or have described to them, the person suspected.

The actual test purchase is carried out as follows:

1. The first person enters the shop and buys several items which add up to a rather large and unusual figure, say £7·14. He or she stands by the till as if just curiously checking that the money is recorded. They also hand bank notes to ensure the need for change and use of the till. We have now succeeded in getting an excellent identifiable mark on the till roll. If they gave you change out of a box and a written receipt from a second receipt book it would obviously be much better evidence. However, in practice, if all the suggested subterfuge is adhered to, they will record the sale in the till.
2. The next operation is where the test comes into force. A second person follows the first, knowing exactly what is to be bought, having exactly the right money ready and not standing near the till. Keeping the exact money ready they wait until the goods are placed in front of them ready to take away. It is at that stage they ask, 'How much?', even though they already know. Pick up the goods, hand over the money and walk naturally but quickly out of the shop. This gives the suspect opportunity to either keep the money or place it in the till.
3. If you are using three people, the next person acts in a similar way to the first, making sure that their purchases are recorded. If the person is dishonest the second sale will not be shown on the roll.

Test purchases are best carried out during lunchtime when the suspect may be in the shop alone.

You will be employed by some companies to carry out regular test purchases at all their branches, not because they suspect dishonesty but merely to ensure a constant vigil. This is a very common security practice and in routine test purchases you may be asked to submit an additional report regarding the smartness and demeanour of staff and general appearance of the shop, etc.

Typists or female operatives can be used to good advantage and are less likely to be suspected.

Upon checking up and finding that the second purchase was not recorded, you have one more piece of excellent evidence. Depending upon the strength of other corroboration you may decide to interview or strengthen the case by further test purchases.

If their guilt is revealed, endeavour to obtain a cautioned statement.

SALESMEN—*Dishonesty*

Cases of dishonesty by salesmen are quite common and, although really a police matter, the private investigator may be instructed in the first instance. This is because a detective agency will usually recover more of the stolen commodity than the police.

A case in point took place some years ago where an outside representative had been selling television sets and faking hire purchase agreements for three months. He was not only getting the cash for the sets, he was also being paid a basic salary and high commission rates. This was inevitably discovered when no instalments were forthcoming on the forged hire purchase agreements and it was handed over to a detective agency.

When interviewed it was eventually admitted that none of his sales were genuine. These amounted to about £1,100. This was a very serious matter for his employer, as all the money had to be re-paid to the hire purchase company, leaving him in dire financial difficulties. The salesman had taken all his names and addresses from the telephone directory, thereby ensuring good status reports when the finance company made their enquiries.

For many hours this smooth, plausible and well-dressed salesman maintained that the goods had been sold to a man called Bill at a bar in the next city. This is the usual type of story proffered, and of course he was not aware of his surname or address!

It was obvious that he was lying, but he did not change his story until about 2.30 p.m. Under caution he then made a statement relating the various second-hand shops, pawnbrokers and dealers where the goods had been sold. All were within the city limits but unfortunately the time was now about 3.30 p.m.

He was obviously a criminal type who could not be released, and would definitely have disappeared by morning. After admitting the true facts he was very co-operative, and from 3.30 p.m. the thief was accompanied from shop to shop, where the situation was explained, and goods to the sum of £300 were recovered. This did not seem serious as the statement showing the goods disposal would be handed to the police and it was reasonable to assume that they would continue recovery on the following day.

The man, together with the property and statement, was handed to the police, when it was found that he was wanted in numerous cities for similar offences. Fortunately his most successful coup was his last, so there could be no question of handing him over to another city.

He was obviously found guilty of the offence and received a prison sentence of six months. The most tragic part was that no further attempts were made to recover the other items, although the private detective agency had found this quite easy and even supplied a full statement incorporating full details of the locations.

FACTORY LARCENY

There are many different versions of this offence and it would be impossible to include them all. Every day people are discovering new ways to steal from factories and almost every offence has some difference in its make-up. The investigator must be alive to this the whole time and be capable in his enquiries of matching the ingenuity of the thief with an equal skill of his own.

Although articles are being stolen it is sometimes absolutely impossible to trace the culprit by the usual methods. In this case it may be advisable to put a man or woman on the inside, working in the department where the thefts occur.

There are various possibilities which will be considered when this type of offence is encountered. These are the same whether the operator is being employed on the inside or not.

1. That the thieves are simply carrying the goods out on their person, in shopping bags, meal containers, etc.
2. Loading the goods into their cars during working hours and driving out at home time.
3. Having a driver as an accomplice. The goods are then loaded in the yard and driven away without suspicion.
4. Articles being pushed through or put over the fence to be collected later.
5. That goods are being allowed to pass through the gates by a dishonest gatekeeper or security guard.

6. The night watchman or security guards could be taking articles during the night.
7. Consider the possible implication of everyone in possession of keys. (Thefts are also committed by 'trusted' employees.)
8. Outside tradesmen working on the premises can often be responsible for theft, e.g. maintenance men, painters, plumbers, etc.

There is no end to the possibilities. This is one instance where the co-operation and advice of a director or manager can be invaluable. They know the system thoroughly and are in a better position to know the different outlets. If a culprit is caught, get the usual cautioned statement and find out the receiver's name.

PAID INFORMANTS

If a paid informant should be used, then make his reward subject to results. It is alright to buy a few drinks, but this type often pretends to possess more information than is actually known, merely to obtain some quick cash. Should the information prove useful then your original offer of money must be honoured. For this type of work a good informant should always be encouraged as he can save days of very laborious routine enquiries.

However, be very careful when dealing with them, honour your obligations but never become too familiar. The very best informant is one who takes a personal liking to you and refuses any remuneration for services rendered. These are very few and far between, but strangely enough they supply the very best information and can always be relied upon.

Remember, never pay an informant except on results. The amount of payment should really be judged on what you will be able to make out of the investigation and will obviously increase accordingly. After they have given successful information and received payment, do not weaken to their entreaties for a loan or they will never be away from the office.

Never reveal the source of information, otherwise your informant will be in hospital for a few months, or even worse. Also, never expect him to be a witness or even suggest the possibility, otherwise you will very quickly lose his services.

10
Industrial Espionage

Industrial espionage is happening more and more frequently as years go by. A fantastic amount of money is both made and lost by the sale of industrial secrets. The type of secrets vary from the grand scale government-sponsored project to the small firm's acquisition of a competitor's list of clients.

There are a few well equipped detective agencies specializing in this type of investigation.

These industrial spies really fall into four categories:

1. The super professional, probably trained at a government spy school.
2. The professional spy, self-employed and fully engaged in this occupation. He may have previously worked for a government, but now sells to the highest bidder.
3. The opportunist. Usually an employee who sells one secret to his employer's competitor, or co-operates with a professional spy.
4. The reporter or journalist who wants the information merely for a good news item.

Although we hear a lot about electronic eavesdropping equipment, in practice not many of these 'bugging' devices are used. They are generally unreliable and produce unsatisfactory results. However, the possibility must never be overlooked in any investigation involving espionage, but usually the professional opts for surer methods than these.

Many weeks will probably be spent in the locality, finding out the habits and weaknesses of employees who work in the department. One of these may eventually be disclosed as a rather weak-willed individual, possibly with something to hide. This is the man the spy is looking for and he will then proceed to put pressure on him. This could be blackmail, but the offer of an attractive cash payment will be the usual method. Once this man has been found and agrees to co-operate, then the rest is quite simple. The spy simply waits for the information, pays the informant and moves on to his next assignment.

An industrial spy will go for anything which can be re-sold, e.g. plans for new designs, details of research work, modifications and technical skill in engines, lists of competitors' clients, new formulas, ideas not yet patented and many others. For years the famous French fashion houses have been desperate to prevent commercial piracy of their exclusive designs prior to their public exhibition, often unsuccessfully.

If instructions are received to carry out this type of work, obtain a full list of all names and addresses relating to:

1. Persons working in the department where leakage occurs.
2. Persons having casual access during the day.
3. Persons responsible for cleaning the department.
4. Persons newly employed since the espionage was first suspected.
5. Persons recently resigned or been dismissed.
6. Persons at executive level who have access to secret information.
7. Persons vaguely suspected by your interviewee.
8. Persons on security staff—provided they have access to the department or to the keys.

In order to compile a character picture of all suspects the investigator should first address his questions to the few high executives and possibly to a limited and carefully selected number of senior employees.

When conducting his enquiries the investigator must not overlook the possibility of an outside person being wholly responsible for the espionage.

Before leaving this subject it will be of interest to note that the best method of procuring secrets and by far the safest, most successful and completely unanswerable, is the enticement of competitors' star employees or executives. They then get the benefit of all his past, present and future endeavours, without recourse to the rather dramatic 'cloak and dagger' methods usually associated with industrial espionage.

11

General Security Measures

It is very difficult to generalize on this subject as all firms, factories and buildings have varied hazards peculiar to themselves. Some firms are security conscious, but others leave themselves wide open for either industrial espionage or physical entry.

All companies should realize that however good the physical security may be, if they have unfaithful or even potentially unfaithful employees on the staff, most other security measures might just as well be abandoned.

Some of the methods mentioned in the following pages will only apply to companies where extreme security measures are absolutely essential.

1. SECURITY CONSCIOUSNESS

The very first thing is to be 'Security Conscious'. Give more thought to this subject and always be on the lookout for new and better ideas.

2. SCREENING EMPLOYEES

Every important employee should be thoroughly screened before employment begins. This does not mean a two line reference from his last employer or the local magistrate, but a full record of all his past employment for the last ten years. The application form should be filled in by a responsible member of the firm whilst interviewing the potential employee, not given to the employee to complete himself.

Apart from the specific details required by a particular firm, for screening purposes, the form should reveal a good deal of the person's personal background and habits, etc.

3. WORKS PASS

Every member of the firm should have a Works Pass, numerically marked and containing a passport-type photograph, with the firm's name stamped over the photograph on to the pass. This avoids the possibility of easily changing the photograph.

4. OUTSIDE TRADESMEN

Great caution should be exercised with outside tradesmen as they represent a weakness to security. It is better for a firm to employ their own maintenance men and window cleaners, etc.

5. DAILY REPORT

A special note should be made by the security staff of any early or late calls made to the works by employees, together with any unusual happenings. This should be in the form of a report, submitted to a senior employee every day, even if negative, when it will merely contain the words 'nothing to report'. These reports can sometimes be very useful and should be filed in date order, even the negative ones.

6. CLASSIFIED DOCUMENTS

Classify all documents. If a file is extremely important then mark it boldly on the outside cover. This is a constant psychological reminder to the authorized few and they will tend to treat the topic with the right degree of respect.

7. CHIEF OF SECURITY

The chief of security should be a man dedicated to his work to the extreme—but he should also be very security minded, attending lectures and visiting security exhibitions, etc., a good leader and disciplinarian and possess the experience which fits him for the post.

Never, under any circumstances, make the ex-gatekeeper into the chief security officer. This is actually the case in many modern firms which have grown with the years. They decide that a more sophisticated form of security is needed so, because of his seniority of service and nothing else, they nominate 'Joe', the old gatekeeper, to lead a bunch of equally inexperienced men; consequently the security is almost non-existent.

8. SECURITY GUARDS

If these are chosen from the ranks of ex-police officers who have served their full term of years and have a discharge certificate showing their conduct as exemplary, then only the minimum amount of screening will be required. On the other hand, if they are younger men, just out of the armed forces or leaving normal civilian occupations, then an absolutely merciless amount of screening is necessary before the guard is accepted. All the guards must have spotless characters as they are in such a vulnerable position of trust. There should also be periodical spot checks on all the guards to ensure their continual blameless demeanour.

These people should be supplied with a smart uniform and receive adequate compensation for the long, irregular hours which they are obliged to work.

9. GUARD DOGS

If there is a large area to cover, guard dogs can be used to excellent advantage, either by roaming at will within the perimeter boundaries or accompanied by a handler. The danger with guard dogs is that some are very badly trained and tend to attack the wrong people. If the local police have dogs, ask their advice relating to what type of dog will be required for your particular circumstances. There is the expensive dog, which is accompanied at all times by a handler and works very expertly under instructions, and there is the vicious brute which roams at will and attacks everything in sight. The latter type is obviously much cheaper and may be more suitable for your purposes. The disadvantage with dogs is that they can easily be drugged.

10. PERIMETER WALLS OR FENCES

For the best security these should be kept in first class repair, being constantly checked for any weaknesses. Certain things present a hazard to the impregnability of boundary walls or fences and these should be avoided if maximum security is to be maintained, e.g. small outbuildings up to the boundary, parked vehicles, a storage dump or abandoned machinery, etc. In fact anything that tends to artificially lessen the true height of the boundary fence on either side.

The gates should be properly manned at all times.

11. FLOODLIGHTS

These are an excellent security measure as thieves are extremely averse to breaking into any type of premises when the area is well lit and they can be discovered much more easily. If possible, the whole perimeter should be floodlit and also the exterior of all buildings, at least where doors and windows are present. They should be set at such an angle that they also throw illumination on to the roof.

The gates should be generously floodlit, enabling the security guards ample vision of persons and vehicles as they are checked in and out.

12. DANGER PERIODS

Very particular attention must be paid to security arrangements at such opportune moments as Christmas, Bank Holidays and all other times when people are absent from work. These are just the periods when the thief is most in need of money, and the industrial spy may anticipate a weakness in security. Skeleton staffs should not be maintained during holidays, even though this may be extremely unpopular with the security guards. This rule applies equally to normal weekends.

The majority of break-in offences occur between 10.30 p.m. and 2.30 a.m., therefore security should be particularly well catered for between these hours.

13. PATROLS

The old idea of night-time patrols by the watchman or security guard, punching a time-clock every hour, on the hour, is definitely out. The more regular the patrols, the more vulnerable are the premises.

Time-clocks are still an excellent idea to ensure full coverage of the premises, but the patrols should be irregular, at the guard's own choice, and no set routes should be maintained.

If the premises close at about 6 p.m. then a full internal search should be undertaken to ensure that no person is hiding on the premises. This search would apply to all outbuildings and any other place of refuge. The same patrol would make a tour of the perimeter to make sure that it was still secure and that everything else was in order. All the windows and doors would be properly secured and perhaps the alarms and floodlights tested. The senior security guard would make a brief report, explaining that everything was in order, or otherwise.

If the chief security officer is efficient he will also be in the habit of making surprise night or early morning visits to the premises, to ensure that his security staff are carrying out their duties correctly and also keep them alert.

14. LOCKS AND SAFES

If maximum security is to be maintained then these two items should be regarded most earnestly when carrying out a full security survey, or merely applying thought to a few improvements.

There are various theories expounded about the merits of both the combination safe and the key safe. The experts will advise you on the different viewpoints and assist in your ultimate decision.

All safe keys should be held personally by responsible members of the firm; never, under any circumstances, should they be left on the premises.

15. WINDOWS

From their very construction, these are obviously the most vulnerable part of any building, and great consideration should be given to their position and security.

Apart from the usual alarm systems, there are various ways of making them less assailable, with particular attention to those situated on the ground floor.

For windows protecting a bank teller or wages clerk, consider the advantages of using unbreakable, or bullet-proof glass. In the few instances where windows must be left open, have louvre windows fitted, thereby ensuring adequate ventilation with the minimum loss of security.

16. BURGLAR ALARMS

These are, without doubt, the best and most modern method of acquiring maximum security. Various alarm systems are on the market, and once again expert advice should be taken before deciding on a particular one.

There are numerous manufacturers of alarm systems involving different types of technical planning to trigger off the contrivance, but only three distinct varieties:

a) The silent warning system which operates when the criminal enters the premises. He is not aware that the alarm has been activated, but a silent signal is passed to the security guards or the police, or both, alerting them of the illegal entry. The principle here is that the building is then surrounded and the intruder caught.

b) The second variety is the type of system of which the criminal is immediately aware. When the alarm operates it is usually in the form of large clanging bells, placed at strategic points on the interior and exterior of the premises. The principle here is to frighten the intruder away, before he accomplishes any further penetration into the building.

c) The third method is exorbitantly expensive and seldom used to cover a whole building, but may be worthy of consideration to protect one eminently important and comparatively small section. This is a system which not only warns the guards and police of the intruder, but also imprisons him within the area which activated the alarm. This is accomplished by the immediate and very swift release of heavy metal grills over all windows and doors, cutting off any means of escape. However, the price of installation is often considered too high to offset against a security precaution.

There are various other alarm systems, designed to protect things other than buildings. These usually come within the definition of paragraph b), for example, security vehicles fitted with alarm bells or sirens; wrist-secured bank messenger's money bag containing a warning bell or siren, which reacts immediately any attempt is made to seize it; alarms fitted to vehicles which react if any would-be thief tried to drive them away. Normal luggage can also be fitted with a burglar alarm. All these systems are excellent security precautions and should be used to the utmost advantage, particularly where money or valuables are in transit.

17. BOARDROOM

The main object here is to attain a level of strict privacy in addition to security and to nullify any possibility of secret information being leaked to an outside source. Unless the strictest methods of security precautions are conscientiously adhered to at all times it is extremely difficult to feel satisfied that this standard is being maintained.

One of the most important precautions is to ensure that no unauthorized person is ever allowed into the boardroom, or ever has the opportunity to plant some bugging device, or a hidden camera.

A thief-proof lock of the very best quality should be fitted and the keys kept at all times in the personal possession of two or three senior executives. The door should be kept locked at all times. All doors and windows should be soundproofed.

18. COLLECTION OF WAGES

In these days, when robberies are happening more and more frequently, the collection of wages in every type of firm presents a security problem that cannot be ignored. The worst possible attitude towards the subject is 'it can never happen to me'. It can happen and most certainly will happen at some future date if adequate precautions are not taken to guard against the possibility.

The extent of these arrangements will obviously depend to a large degree on the size of the pay-roll, but whether for a small concern or a large industrial plant with thousands of workers, some proportionate security measures must be employed.

If the firm has about forty employees, then it would be worthwhile to have an alarmed valise and also an adult male to accompany the carrier.

With any pay-roll larger than this, some definite and more organized form of security should be practised. Imagination should be applied to the subject by every person connected with the perilous occupation of collecting vast amounts of money and being responsible for them during transit.

Time of collection

Possibly the greatest error to avoid is habituation. The times for collecting the wages should be altered each week.

Bank and Route

The police in most districts tend to have a constable present outside each bank during the drawing of wages, but this does not mean that vigilance can be relaxed. On the contrary, this may be exactly what the criminals anticipate and the actual transfer of monies from the bank to the vehicle is the period most fraught with danger. This is the only time that the money is actually in the open and relieves the assailants of having to forcibly immobilize the vehicles. Constantly change route from bank to destination.

19. MISCELLANEOUS SECURITY MEASURES

a) In some cases it may be advisable to have a works ruling to forbid cameras.
b) Ensure that authorized personnel wear special badges before entering restricted areas.
c) Always be particularly aware of the risk of entry from adjoining premises. Their security may be very lax compared to yours.
d) Make certain that there are no joint underdrawings or easy access by the cellar.
e) The roof should be regarded as a hazard and made equally as impregnable as other areas.
f) Anything open to aerial photography should be covered or camouflaged.
g) Where applicable, check the security of the printing or advertising organization dealing with the firm's business.
h) Never use over dramatic or exaggerated methods of security as these will be taken in the wrong spirit and the guards will tend to ignore them. Base all ideas on sound common sense.
i) The best method of preventing a wages attack is to pay by cheque!

j) Guard dogs might accompany wages vehicles.
k) Never keep the wages at the firm overnight.

There are numerous other security precautions which will apply to the particular premises and needs of the individual involved. When carrying out a security survey the private investigator must be very thorough and must not overlook any of the possibilities mentioned here, but in addition he must not fail to notice other possible hazards.

The whole concept of security should be to hinder the progress of the criminal. It may be literally impossible to stop them gaining entry, or attacking, but at every stage they should be faced with as many security obstacles as modern methods can devise. If this is accomplished, then the security is sound and the criminal will probably be either caught in the act or abandon the project in disgust.

12
Giving Evidence

GENERAL

To be a competent private investigator one of the most important qualifications is to recount the details of evidence in a clear, honest manner, leaving the court in no doubt as to its authenticity. To do this it is not necessary to repeat the proof like a parrot. The evidence should be given more or less in accordance with the statement (or Proof of Evidence) sent to the solicitors, and the investigator should have a good grasp of all the material background details which may be associated with it. The judge, or the defence, may ask questions having no bearing on the evidence given by you, e.g. type of house, can you recall someone calling whilst you were there, what was in the vacant bedrooms, etc. These questions are often quite relevant to some point introduced into the case from another source and, as you are the expert witness, the court often asks the question in order to clear up some ambiguity. Before the case have a good look at the file, recalling the interview and surroundings, which will usually be sufficient to refresh your memory enough to answer any other questions which may arise.

There is a definite atmosphere of traditional pomp and ceremony in most courts and, if anything, it will be this awesome grandeur that upsets the newcomer. This is easily overcome by being a constant spectator in the local courts. In this way the atmosphere and procedure will be very quickly familiarized and at the same time you will be able to observe exactly how evidence is given by other private investigators and police witnesses.

When a private investigator attends court to give evidence,

it is just another part of his working day and whilst it is an extremely important part of his occupation, it must not be treated with an exaggerated reverence to the exclusion of everything else.

In an undefended divorce petition, the investigator sits in court the whole time. When the case is called the first witness is the petitioner, whose evidence is usually quite short and then the investigator may be called. He should walk quietly into the witness box and immediately taking the Bible in his ungloved right hand, take the oath.

Spoken words should always be modulated to suit the circumstances, but they must at all times be spoken in a clear tone, capable of reaching not only the persons in the immediate vicinity but the whole courtroom. It is most embarrassing for a professional witness to be told by the judge or barrister to speak up. The whole of the evidence should be directed towards the judge even though the questions may be coming from the barristers or solicitors.

Be in sympathy with the shorthand writer who has to take down a verbatim record of the proceedings, later producing a full transcript of the case for official records. Whether shorthand, a shorthand machine or longhand is used, make sure that you are not galloping ahead or they will be forced to interrupt you. A pause at the end of long passages helps, glancing at the writer for a nod to proceed.

EVIDENCE

This evidence will be made up of notes at the time of interview or during the course of the investigation. Providing the notes were made at the time or as soon afterwards as possible, then the private investigator is quite in order to refer to these notes whilst giving evidence. (The same rule applies to a constable's notebook.)

The professional witness is, therefore, left with a choice of two alternatives. Either he wastes hours of valuable time swotting up to become word perfect and give his evidence without any reference to notes, or he has a quick look at the notes before entering court to refresh his memory of the circumstances and gives his evidence in a quietly efficient manner, not actually reading the notes, but using them as a constant reminder of what to say next. However, he should read verbatim all the actual replies made by the accused in direct speech. The author once gave evidence on about twenty occasions in one day; the length of the evidence was equivalent to about two Shakespearian plays, which would have been great fun to try and learn by heart!

The recommended method of giving evidence is to stand in the box with a smart, relaxed bearing; the investigation file open at the original notes, held at about waist level, facing the judge or chairman; and speaking in a distinct, unhurried manner, alternating vision in turn towards the notes, the judge and the shorthand writer.

A familiar question is, 'What are those notes to which you refer?' The answer is, 'These are the notes made by me at the time of the original interview.'

If you are referring to notes, the court or defence have the right, if granted by the judge, to examine them. However, if they were made honestly at the time and the contents are genuine, then they will, if anything, tend to strengthen the prosecution's or petitioner's case.

Do not have the mistaken impression that you will be granted any special treatment or favours by the court. You are merely another witness for one side or the other, perhaps even more suspect because you will probably be the only paid witness. Because of this it is even more important that all evidence is unquestionably correct and all defence questions are answered fairly, trying to be as impartial as the circumstances allow, without detriment to your client's case if the evidence clearly points in his favour.

When you have taken the oath, wait for your barrister to lead into the evidence, first by saying something similar to 'Are you Edward Collins, a private investigator carrying on business at .... address .... under the name of .... Detective Agency?', to which the reply would be, 'Yes, sir.'

It is at this stage of the evidence that the investigator forms his opinion of how that particular barrister intends to present his evidence to the court, and sympathetically adapts his style of giving evidence to that obviously preferred by the barrister, thereby ensuring a smooth flow of evidence rather than a jumbled mass created by the investigator and the barrister fighting each other to present the evidence in their own way. Quite unintentionally this often occurs and creates embarrassment for both parties, with the judge striving to make sense of the minor chaos which this type of clash creates.

The barrister has your original statement in front of him and as this has been dictated from your notes at the time of interview, the contents of both will be identical. The evidence is given in the form of this statement, therefore the sequence of the evidence is sure. This is not where the confusion arises, but rather in how the barrister is to extract the contents and present them to the court. After this initial period of introduction one barrister may simply say, 'Would you give your evidence to the court?', afterwards merely clearing up any points that are ambiguous or have been forgotten. Another barrister may prefer to lead throughout the whole testimony, e.g. 'At .... time and date .... you went to .... address .... Who did you see there?' The investigator would then recount the names and his mode of identification, although the barrister might even lead to the extent of saying, 'How did you identify these people?'

He could then continue, 'What did you then say to them?', following with, 'What did Mr .... reply?', then, 'And what did Miss .... reply?'

The investigator must anticipate the barrister's wishes, otherwise his evidence and the barrister's questions will constantly override each other with the confusion increasing, alternating between deathly silences and two clashing voices. If the investigator wishes to be regarded as a good professional witness, he should not have his own method of giving testimony, but learn to sense immediately what method is favoured by the barrister and follow this smoothly throughout.

If the case is defended, the investigator will then be cross-examined. There may be an attack here, but all questions should be answered by 'yes' or 'no' where possible. After this comes the re-examination by the investigator's own barrister, based on the facts revealed by the cross-examination.

When both barristers have finished the judge may want to ask further questions, so do not leave the box until you receive his indication to do so.

ANSWERING QUESTIONS

From whatever source these come, listen carefully and understand the question. If necessary ask the questioner to repeat it. If the answer is not known, never try to bluff it out, simply say that you do not know. If you should have known the answer, precede the phrase with a very short apology.

It has been said that the most difficult witness to cross-examine is the one who constantly answers merely 'yes' or 'no'. Without any doubt this is the proper way to deal with cross-examination. Avoid at all costs the traps set by the defence counsel, who constantly tries to lead you into long complicated explanations, thereby supplying him with further ammunition to continue his verbal attack.

Always be civil and never be provoked into losing your temper. Equally, never give way to mirth, although on occasions this may be a most difficult object to suppress. Avoid any desire to be dramatic, keeping evidence and answers in simple, everyday language.

MISCELLANEOUS

1. When the judge or chairman of any court enters or rises to leave, everyone stands up and keeps silent.
2. Avoid loud whispered conversations with colleagues, if you must talk keep it down to a very low whisper.
3. Walk quietly in a courtroom.
4. Always look at the list displayed outside the court to ascertain the sequence of the cases and be ready in the court when your case is called. For various reasons, cases are often taken completely out of sequence, so never leave the court thinking that you have time for a coffee. Even if you leave the actual courtroom, always stay close enough to hear your name if called.
5. If a point is raised at the hearing which you can clear up, write a quick note or have a whispered conversation with your solicitor or his clerk, never with the barrister unless you happen to be temporarily standing in for the solicitor.
6. Always treat the court and presiding authority with the traditional deference and respect to which they are entitled. However, do not become overawed as this will only lead to inefficiency.
7. Smoking is not allowed in a courtroom and upon entering, all males must remove their hats.
8. Always arrive at the court at least ten or fifteen minutes before

the proceedings are due to begin. This enables you to calmly sort out your cases and leaves time to possibly have a brief word with the solicitor or barrister.
9. Offensive language in evidence should be written out and handed to the clerk or usher.

13
Laws of Evidence and Procedure

INTRODUCTION

These laws or principles have taken centuries to formulate and are the rules that ensure justice is done. Every investigator must have a sound knowledge of these rules and their meanings, as he is the person responsible for collecting evidence and later presenting it to the court. A court of law enquires into crime and civil offences of all types, their object being to establish either the guilt or innocence of the accused, and this guilt or innocence is established by means of evidence.

EVIDENCE DEFINED

Evidence is: That which makes a fact evident.
That which supplies proof.
The means by which any point may be proved or disproved.

Legal
Definition: The term 'evidence' is used to indicate the means by which any fact or point in issue, or question may be proved or disproved in a manner complying with the legal rules governing the subject.

TYPES OF EVIDENCE

Oral Evidence
A witness relating the facts verbally.

Documentary Evidence

A document produced in court, usually proved by a witness as authentic, e.g. medical certificate, photograph, cheque, plan or sketch, statement, marriage certificate, birth certificate, account books, etc.

Real Evidence

This includes articles used in or connected with the circumstances of the offence. They will always prove extremely useful in the petitioner's or prosecution's case, e.g. stained garments, weapons, breaking implements, or stolen property.

Circumstantial Evidence (Sometimes called Presumptive Evidence)

This is evidence, not of the actual fact to be proved, but of circumstances from which that fact can be inferred with more or less certainty; e.g. stolen goods on suspected thief; fibres or hairs on suspect's clothing; murderer's scarf found round neck of victim.

Circumstantial evidence often predominates in felonies and murder enquiries as these are seldom actually seen being committed.

Primary Evidence (Often referred to as 'Direct' or 'Positive' Evidence)

This is, without doubt, the very best type of evidence of a fact actually perceived by a witness by means of any of his senses, i.e. taste, smell, sight, hearing or feeling. This also includes the production by a witness of an original document.

Secondary Evidence

If primary evidence of a fact is not available, then it is necessary to produce the best alternative, which is termed 'secondary evidence'; e.g. deposition or statement of a witness who, by means of his senses, would be able to give primary evidence, but is not able to attend court through illness, etc.; copy of a document; a model of something which cannot be moved.

N.B. Before Secondary Evidence will be accepted by the court it must be proved to their satisfaction that the Primary

Evidence is not available, e.g. witness died or document destroyed.

Opinion Evidence

Very seldom admissible in evidence, but the following are certain exceptions to this rule, usually called expert witnesses.

1. In matters of science, profession or trade, an expert may be asked for his opinion as to the consequences of a fact already proved in evidence.
2. Handwriting or finger-print experts.
3. Where the identity of a person is in dispute.
4. Reference regarding general character of accused.
5. Expert opinion regarding literary, artistic, scientific or other meritorious worth of articles, subject of obscenity charge.

Hearsay Evidence

Could be loosely termed 'second-hand' evidence and is very seldom admissible.

Definition: This is the evidence given by a witness, of what he heard another person (not the defendant) say.

This evidence is usually inadmissible because:

1. What the other person said was not on oath.
2. The defendant had no opportunity of cross-examination.

Exceptions where hearsay evidence may be given:

1. Dying declarations.
2. Early complaint of victim to another in cases of rape, incest, indecent assault, etc. (This will negate the defendant's defence of the victim's consent.)
3. Records and statements of deceased persons in course of business.
4. Statement as to bodily feelings, e.g. in a poisoning case, the words spoken by the deceased to another about the pains in his stomach.
5. When the hearsay comes in as part of the *res gestae*, i.e. things done or incidents relevant to the matter in issue. Possibly not quite accurate to describe this as hearsay, but it does come within the definition; e.g. in a case of manslaughter, the spoken words by the deceased about the cause of death.
6. To confirm or invalidate oral testimony. What a witness has said previously to some other person may be admissible to prove

or disprove the truth of his testimony. (A good example would be the previously mentioned Negative Statement.)
7. Relating to Old Customs and Public Rights. Elderly witnesses might be called to recount what they heard in their youth from other persons, now deceased.
8. Death beyond the sea. Witnesses can be called to prove this fact, even though the evidence is hearsay.
9. Declarations against the pecuniary or proprietary interest of the deceased. Declarations by deceased persons may be given in evidence, e.g. that he was illegitimate, or an entry in deceased's books that payment to the deceased had been made, or that he possessed a rent book, therefore the property was not his.

Corroborative Evidence

This is other independent evidence that tends to support the truthfulness and accuracy of evidence already given. Corroborative evidence is required by law in cases of perjury, procuration and of the unsworn evidence of children of tender years.

COMPETENCY OF WITNESSES

This question is decided by the court, but the general rule is that all persons are quite competent to give evidence in all cases. However, the court may regard a witness as incompetent if they decide that *a)* they lack discretion, e.g. drunken person, lunatic or idiot; *b)* a child of tender years, if the court decides that he is too young to have sufficient intelligence to understand his duty to tell the truth; *c)* generally the husband or wife of the accused, although there are certain exceptions.

A child of tender years may give evidence, even if he is too young to understand the meaning of the oath, providing they satisfy the court that they understand their duty to speak the truth. (This evidence must be corroborated.)

The principal accessory or accomplice to an offence may also give evidence.

WITNESSES OUT OF COURT

At the request of the prosecution or defence, the court may order all witnesses to give evidence out of court. This prevents them being influenced by hearing what the other witnesses have to say. If a witness then remains in court his evidence will not be rejected, but he may be punished for contempt.

INTERFERENCE WITH WITNESSES

It is an offence to dissuade, hinder or prevent any witness from attending court, providing he has been summoned or bound over by recognizance. The attempt is a similar offence. Any interference with witnesses lays the offender open to a charge of contempt.

HOSTILE WITNESS

If a witness shows himself to be opposed to the side calling him the court may give permission for him to be treated as a hostile witness.

If a counsel is granted this permission he may:

1. Put leading questions to the witness.
2. Cross-examine him.
3. Contradict him by means of other evidence.
4. Prove that he has previously made a statement inconsistent with his present testimony, but he must first be asked if he made such a statement.

PRIVILEGE

This is claimed by certain witnesses as a right, i.e. that they may decline to give evidence on certain matters. The following examples are privileged:

1. Husband/wife of defendant.
2. Witness is not bound to answer incriminating questions but this does not apply to accused giving testimony on his own behalf.
3. Lawyer of defendant.
4. Privilege can be claimed by a witness regarding the production of official documents, if disclosure would be against the public interest or injurious to a public service.
5. A police officer, private investigator or reporter may ask for the name of his informant to be privileged, on the grounds that it would put the man in grave danger from reprisal, etc., but the name must be revealed if the information is material or necessary in the interest of the accused and the judge so orders.

The following are not privileged, although they are commonly thought to be so:

1. Doctor and patient. Irrespective of their confidential relationship, they are definitely not privileged.
2. Priest in confessional. In practice the priest may not be called upon to reveal a confession, but he is definitely not privileged by right.

LEADING QUESTIONS

These are questions so framed as to suggest to the witness the desired answer or which contain the answer and can usually be answered by 'yes' or 'no'.

Leading questions may not be put to a witness by the side producing him, except for convenience. The following are examples of the occasions when leading questions are permitted:

1. On all introductory matters, name and address, etc.
2. For the purpose of identifying persons or things, e.g. an exhibit or identifying the prisoner, etc.
3. When called to contradict the testimony of previous witness.
4. Hostile witness.

A witness recounting complicated matters, or whose memory fails, can be asked questions of such a nature to lead the mind of the witness back to the subject. These are not really leading questions, but could probably be better described as 'prompting' questions.

14
Service of Legal Process

GENERAL

This is quite a straightforward subject, providing the process server keeps to the rules and follows his instructions to the letter. If any writ or summons is encountered which presents problems, then merely ring up the instructing solicitor for clarification. All private investigators handle a good deal of legal documents in various actions, or matters relevant to claims, or court proceedings being pursued by their clients. The investigator usually hands a true copy (sometimes an original) of a document to a person—called 'serving'—and in this capacity he is known as a Process Server. The remaining document is then endorsed as to the time and place of service and the endorsement signed, e.g. 'Edward Collins, Process Server'.

With another process, the form of endorsement could be printed at the foot of the document, leaving the process server to fill in the blank spaces. On others, this is not present and the whole wording of the endorsement must be typed and signed, usually on the rear of the remaining document, often the original, but sometimes the copy. The wording of the endorsement will be similar to the following:

.... date ....

A true copy of the within (Originating Summons, Order, Subpoena, etc.) together with (any accompanying documents) was served by me upon the (Defendant, Respondent, Witness, etc.) John Smith, at .... time, day, date and place ....

Signed: Edward Collins, Process Server
Address ....

If the original document was to be served, the wording of the endorsement would commence:

The original of the within (............) of which this is a true copy, was served by me .... etc. ....

N.B. It is preferable for all endorsements to be completed immediately after service as the solicitors cannot proceed until the document is returned to their possession. Always check the copy document against the original and if incorrect return to the solicitor for amendment.

If various persons are named on the original document, with copies for each, then separate endorsements must be entered for each service.

The biggest crime a process server can commit is to serve the original document instead of the copy, or vice versa. If this should happen, then try to retrieve the document, exchanging it for the correct one. If it is not possible to recover the wrongly served document, immediately inform the solicitors who may be able to take certain action to rectify the matter.

CONDUCT MONEY

As the name suggests, this is money handed to a person at the time of service to ensure his appearance at the hearing, to be used for travelling expenses and sometimes subsistence. It is usually handed to witnesses when serving a subpoena or witness summons and in some other cases.

It is important to obtain some form of receipt for the money, even if it is only a very small amount, and where a printed form of acknowledgement is not present on the documents, in addition to the normal endorsement wording, at the end—before the signature—add:

'At the time of service I handed to Mr Smith the sum of £1·00 (One pound) Conduct Money'.

Signed

The conduct money must be paid or tendered at the time of service and if this is refused, the fact should be included in the endorsement.

Conduct money is defined as 'a reasonable and sufficient sum of money to defray the expense of coming and attending to give evidence and of returning from giving evidence'.

In certain actions, the defendant or witness may be local and the money may be only for bus fares, but in other cases it could be several pounds for return train fares with an additional sum for transport at both ends of the journey, meals and perhaps even enough for overnight accommodation.

This money has nothing whatever to do with fees for attendance or loss of earnings. These questions will be dealt with later, possibly decided upon at the hearing; but in any case the witness can be assured that a fair and reasonable assessment is always made, ensuring that they do not lose money by their attendance.

PERSONAL SERVICE

This only includes serving a document on a person and does not apply to service upon companies. Very few services present any problems, one simply approaches the person, ensures that he is the correct party and hands over the document.

It is more usual to serve a copy, but the original must always be available at the time of service in order that this can be produced to the person on his request. It is because the process server must, by law, carry the original that mistakes are sometimes made, but there can be no valid argument against this ruling as the person served obviously has a perfect right to demand proof that the copy is genuine. In practice most people accept the copy without question but they do sometimes ask for sight of the original.

To make what is termed a 'good service' it is only necessary to touch some part of the individual's body with the actual document. Therefore, if a person refuses to accept the process in his hand—and this does happen—then tuck the paper in his coat or touch his shoulder with it. Even if he throws it away or lets it fall to the ground, or throws it back at you, do not retrieve it. Although not satisfactory, the service is 'good' and will be accepted by the court. It may be torn to shreds in your presence, thrown away, or if the person receiving the document runs away you may only be able to touch his retreating figure with it, but even these services will be accepted, being the only method available. In the event that you explained through a closed door the contents of a legal document to the person named in the action, if he refused to open the door, the document could be left on the step and this would probably be regarded as a 'good' service.

On average, about one in thirty services seems to be awkward and about one in three hundred may contain minor ingredients of physical assault or attempted assault upon the process server. These are ridiculous, embarrassing and utterly uncalled for situations, as the contents of the document served, whether the recipient regards them as unfair or not, have nothing whatever to do with the process server. However, the odd person will not accept this, he gets into a rage either because he has eventually been served or because of hatred for the person issuing the process, and attempts to vent his feelings on the uninvolved and completely innocent go-between. On the very isolated occasions when this happens, firstly make sure that the document is served and then get out of the way with as much dignity as possible. If it should be impossible to avoid an out and out brawl, then the writer would only proffer one piece of advice—make sure that you win!

When any of these incidents arise, then it would appear almost certain that the recipient is not going to obey or acknowledge the contents of the document, therefore an affidavit will usually be sworn to establish proof of service. In view of this, when returning the remaining document to the solicitor, accompany it with a short statement setting out the details of what took place, with particular reference to how the service was actually effected, e.g. 'the defendant was running away, but I was able to touch him on the right shoulder with the copy .... which then fell to the ground. Mr Smith must have been aware of this but as I then left the scene I do not know whether he returned to collect the document or not.'

These details can then be included in the affidavit of service. There are numerous other cases where an affidavit is sworn, not having any connection with awkward services, but merely as proof of service.

ALLEGED PAYMENT OF CLAIM

It may happen that a defendant, upon being served, will show receipts or apparent proof that the matter referred to in the document has been settled; the document must still be served and the process server must not be influenced to take it back. When a person is served he may suggest that he prefers his solicitor to accept service, but he should still be served personally and advised to send it along to his solicitor.

WRONG NAMES OR DESCRIPTIONS

Alterations must never be made to any document, except by the court, where a certain procedure is followed and the amendment sealed. When any mistake is encountered in the spelling of the surname, first names, wrong initials or wrong descriptions, such as married woman, widow, etc.; the document must not be served but returned to the solicitors for amendment.

This does not apply to a wrong address but the change of address must be shown either in the endorsement or your accompanying letter.

GENERAL

The process server will constantly encounter numerous documents which he may never have seen before. However, the letter of instruction from solicitors will usually contain the guide as to which part should be served and the document itself may reveal a good deal of information. If the position is still not clear—and this is not uncommon—take further instruction rather than create a good deal of unnecessary trouble.

As a general rule service cannot be effected on Sunday, Good Friday or Christmas Day.

FOREIGN PROCESS

At infrequent intervals the process server may receive documents for service which come from abroad. When this happens, work according to the instructing letter. However, if the information is not absolutely clear, have a friendly discussion about it with your own solicitor or contact the legal representative of the issuing country's embassy.

CHARGES

Will vary according to the area and number of visits, etc.

15
Commencing in Business

OFFICE, CLIENTS AND ADMINISTRATION

Commencing in business is the boldest and most frightening step of all. Great consideration is necessary before taking this decision and one should reflect very deeply before making it, particularly upon the old and very true adage, 'Walk before you can run'.

It is neither anticipated nor advocated that a person should read this book one day and start up his own agency the next. This might be possible for an ex-policeman or an existing private investigator—even if he is only working part-time—but some slight experience of the occupation is preferable in order to get the 'feel' of the investigation world. On the other hand, there may be exceptions to this rule and the writer, bearing this in mind, has tried throughout to portray a practical picture.

Accepting and digesting the above comments, it is equally true to say that some carefully calculated risks must be taken, otherwise nothing is ever achieved and one stays in a rut for the rest of one's life. However, make sure that the three words 'carefully calculated risks' are not mistaken for the words 'reckless gamble'.

Before a final decision is reached, certain rather obvious points should be reflected upon:

1. After paying for the fixtures, fittings, furniture and equipment, is there sufficient remaining capital to pay all the rent, rates, gas, electricity, insurance, cleaners, advertising, motoring expenses, National Insurance stamps, printing and stationery bills, postage, window cleaners, telephone accounts, wages and

personal drawings for at least a year. (Private investigator's accounts are seldom paid by return and this amount of capital is therefore required until money starts to come in.)
2. Has the area a sufficient number of established and respected agencies or is there room for one more? (If it is possible to give a better service, then even if there are enough agencies it might be a worthwhile risk to contemplate.)
3. A private investigator should not only be a first class detective if he is to succeed, he must also be a first class businessman. Are both these qualities within the scope of the new investigator?
4. Is the investigator aware of the long hard hours involved if a good living is to be earned, and this sometimes includes all the recognized national holidays?
5. Has the investigator the right type of wife who will make allowances for the enforced absences from home, and is he himself prepared to abandon a normal family life?
6. Is the investigator quite sure that he is not regarding the occupation in a wrongly adventurous and romantic fashion? If so, a very rude awakening is in store.
7. Has he considered that by the time he is fifty the life may become too hard, leaving him with no qualifications for any other type of work? (This would not apply if a good staff was employed, but upon being trained they often leave to start up on their own.)
8. A busy private investigator's social life is almost non-existent, not by choice but by necessity.
9. Is the investigator prepared to spend a good 50 per cent of his time dealing with matrimonial troubles? (There is certainly nothing wrong with this but nevertheless it would not be suitable for everyone.)
10. Does the investigator possess the strength of character necessary to carry out his duties efficiently, without personal corruption to his own morals? This is a most difficult commodity to accurately define, but should incorporate absolute and utter loyalty to his clients and their best interests; honesty and fairness towards the involved parties, with a strong unshakeable integrity, which will not allow sentimentality to encroach upon his reasoning when presented with a particularly unpleasant task.

Having decided in favour of your own agency, the next step is to find suitable office accommodation. Ideally this should be in the same area as the solicitors, which in most cities is usually near the courts. Presumably funds will be limited, therefore moderately priced accommodation is necessary and the cheapest is usually rather dilapidated, but can be marvellously improved with a little do-it-yourself decoration. Keep well away from the new office blocks as these are far too expensive and a further disadvantage is the usual inclusion in the lease of a restrictive clause that tenants must vacate their offices by 6 p.m. If possible, an investigator should try to have offices where he has official access at all times. If a secretary is employed or visualized in the near future, then a private office with a smaller office and waiting room would be necessary. It may work out cheaper to lease a large room and have it partitioned to fit these requirements.

By choice the private office should not lead off the waiting room as people sometimes have an annoying habit of barging straight in, perhaps when an important discussion is in progress.

When considering furnishings, unless you have plenty of capital, the best method is to buy these either from the salerooms or the second-hand furnishing shops. Never take advantage of offers to completely furnish the whole place on a rental agreement, or strangle yourself with hire purchase commitments. It is much better to buy outright carefully chosen and reasonably matching items thereby keeping overheads down to a minimum.

Books kept could be a double entry cash book and ledger. At the beginning, a good qualified firm of accountants should be chosen and, if asked, they will be pleased to show the investigator how to keep these books and also the secrets of P.A.Y.E. A petty cash book, stamp book and day book might also be used, the last showing what is being earned from each different type of enquiry.

A few good law books are absolutely essential, say one used by most police officers, one on divorce, one on evidence and procedure, the last one on crime. This is the minimum and advice about a choice could be sought from a good law bookshop, but preferably from your solicitor.

Reading a Law Book

First study the table of contents and get a general idea of the layout.

Carefully study:	1. The table of statutes. 2. The table of cases. 3. The index.

Learn the abbreviations if any given.

Reading Law:	This is a difficult subject to digest and very careful perusal is necessary. Many Acts contain their own interpretations and definitions.
Be aware of:	Alternatives—OR Attendant circumstances—AND Discretion—MAY Obligation—MUST or SHALL Provisos—EXCEPTIONS to the RULE.
Definitions:	Good preliminary study. No good learning them mechanically. Meaning should be clearly understood as they contain certain requirements in law.
Essential Equipment:	Car, camera with flash, binoculars and possibly a tape recorder. There is much more sophisticated equipment now available, but these few items will certainly suffice in the beginning.

HOW TO FIND CLIENTS

At first, one is obviously prepared to take on any type of work, however small, and it will be the manner in which this work is dealt with which may lead to more remunerative assignments. The first step is to make everyone aware of your existence. An interesting circular should be thoughtfully composed, setting out the aims and type of work you hope to deal in; it could also contain a list of charges. The first batch would be sent to the solicitors, followed up by personal visits. Always ask to speak to the person dealing with divorce and general court work.

After all the solicitors have been circularized and seen, next would come the local business people and accountants, who may be able to supply debt collecting and tracing work. A different circular would probably be used for this last group.

Local advertising in the press would be carried out to attract private clients.

If all these things are accomplished the agency, with a little luck, should now be dealing with enquiries and a successful start to a new career has been made.

ADMINISTRATION

This is the one subject which, simply by itself, can make or break any office which provides some kind of professional service to the public, yet many offices fail to grasp this point and unknowingly lose a tremendous amount of potential business.

Female Employees

It would be no good being a brilliant detective if the girl answering the 'phone fails to take messages, forgets names, does not make proper appointments, or treats clients in an off-hand manner.

The first essential, therefore, must be a really good, keen, secretary/receptionist, with a pleasant manner, who is able to deal with clients over the telephone or to callers at the office.

She must be trained to:

1. Answer the 'phone correctly.
2. When the investigator is out and a potential client telephones or calls, she must take the diary and make a definite appointment for later in the day, or at the earliest convenient time for the client and her employer. (If she merely says, 'Oh, can you ring, or call, back this afternoon? Mr .... will be in then', the agency would never hear from that person again, for a more competent agency would be contacted.)
3. Be most discreet with her questioning and cease if the other party obviously finds it embarrassing. She may enquire into why a client requires the agency's assistance as some guide for her employer's benefit, e.g. matrimonial enquiry, missing person, etc., but only AFTER a proper appointment has been made.
4. As Saturday morning is the busiest time of the week, she must be prepared to work until 12.30 p.m.
5. She should be able to differentiate between the very important client who warrants V.I.P. treatment and the troublesome chap with one small trace, who thinks this entitles him to regard the office as his second home.
6. She must be capable of discretion and must never even hint at what past or present cases have been or are being handled by the agency. There would be no harm in relating the odd amusing

story, providing nothing was said to identify the persons or company involved, although it would really be much better if the girl just refused to discuss the office. This applies equally to the investigator and any other members of the staff.

The secretary/receptionist in a one-man agency becomes an extremely important person, because the whole office is literally in her charge for a good proportion of every working day and if she is a capable, loyal girl, who handles everything quietly but efficiently, she becomes almost indispensable. She should therefore be paid a salary in excess of the normal local rates, thereby rewarding her virtues and, one hopes, retaining her services.

The writer employed four girls in the office and, without exception, they all agreed that their work in a detective agency was totally different to any other office work which they had previously encountered. The variety of assignments made their working days interesting rather than the usual mundane routine that is customary in some offices. Some of these girls became quite expert in dealing with test purchases, and many enjoyable nights were spent by the whole staff, detectives and secretaries, invading an area to obtain signatures for some petition or other, and the girls always got more signatures than the hard-bitten detectives!

Many agencies also employ female operatives, dealing mostly with observations, test purchases and undercover assignments in ladies' salons or other firms where females are employed. They may also take divorce statements. Some agencies are owned and operated very successfully by women.

Male Employees

These people can really be a problem as, unlike other occupations, a capable private investigator cannot be found by advertising in the local press. They have to be recruited in a completely raw state and moulded into some semblance of what the employment demands. This book may help in altering this situation.

As stated earlier in these pages, a good police detective would not necessarily be a good private investigator unless he appreciated the finer points of the occupation, was also a good businessman, learned further law to adapt his skill to civil matters, and finally was not past the age when he was prepared to work night and day on behalf of his clients. If all these further qualities were present, then he would probably become an excellent private investigator, as there is no doubt that in many ways the two occupations are parallel.

Apart from regular staff who handle the more important assignments, most agencies will also employ several part-time men and women to carry out enquiries fitting in with their irregular hours. Some of these will be in occupations not even remotely connected with detective work, but some may be employed in a vaguely similar capacity, for some government department or furniture store. Never, under any circumstances, employ a person who also currently works for another detective agency. This would be tantamount to business suicide for two agencies will often be dealing with one enquiry, but on opposite sides of the fence.

Further full-time staff will usually be recruited from amongst the best of these part-timers, or perhaps from members of the local police force who contact the agency from time to time in the hope of a full-time job.

The good private investigators seem to stay just long enough to be properly trained and then leave to open up their own agency. In a way one cannot blame the last type, but unfortunately they usually go before the employer has managed to recoup his losses on the six or eight months' initial training. In many ways an agency is cutting its own throat by training future competitors, but the only alternative is to stay a one-man business forever. Service agreements are often used to keep some control over staff, but in practice they are seldom enforced as this means unpleasant and embarrassing litigation in the local court.

Owners of detective agencies are already aware of this unfortunate situation, but any would-be employer is now fully warned of what sort of problems to expect.

As a matter of interest, the writer was never employed by an agency, but commenced trading on his own account immediately upon his resignation from the Police Service.

Correspondence

Always send separate letters for separate enquiries; never include other information as the letter cannot be torn in half for inclusion in two files.

When writing a letter, always try to put yourself in the other party's shoes, neither ramble on at great length about unimportant matters, nor almost repeat in a letter the whole context of the accompanying report. It is sufficient to say that you are enclosing the report. Anything else in the letter should refer to items not included in the report.

If an outgoing letter is requesting a reference or any other favour upon which a reply is desired, always enclose a stamped addressed envelope for the reply.

All matters should be religiously acknowledged on the day of receipt.

If any matter is being delayed or causing particular difficulties, then submit either an interim report or a letter explaining the circumstances, giving your views and asking for further instructions. Never put the file on one side and conveniently forget about it.

Always be absolutely certain that the correct documents are put in the appropriate envelopes.

If a letter appears to read ambiguously have it retyped properly. This also applies when there have been a lot of alterations, for a good standard of paper work should be maintained at all times and anything which is not presentable should not be allowed to leave the office.

Income Tax

A regular reserve of money must be placed on one side for this purpose. More small businesses seem to court trouble by this single oversight than any other. The demand will be sent by the Inland Revenue each year and it must be paid. Bear this in mind when there appears to be plenty of money in the bank and you are considering office renovations, new equipment or expensive holidays.

Annual Holidays

For many weeks in advance enclose complimentary slips with every envelope, giving out a short typed message setting out the dates, e.g. 'Closed for annual holidays 19th August to 4th September'. If possible, both principal and secretary should take their holidays during the same period, but this would not apply if many staff were involved; a rota system could then be used and the office would stay open.

Debtors

After repeated reminders, if people still refuse payment, make a list every three or four months for your solicitor's attention.

SPARE-TIME EMPLOYMENT

Providing the person is competent, almost any assignment may be undertaken. With some occupations, say a self-employed insurance agent, even enquiries involving court appearances can be included. However, the first problem is to find some employment and this is usually accomplished by approaching a local detective agency and offering to carry out work on their behalf. If you have a motor-car and seem capable, then the agency will often be only too pleased to utilize your services. It is also useful if the agency is able to contact you by telephone.

Initially you may only be trusted with simple and comparatively easy debt tracings, or perhaps a few straightforward observations; but in a short time you would no doubt be serving legal process and even taking part in the more interesting investigations which require more skill and careful judgement.

A woman can be just as efficient, and many agencies would be prepared to offer a trial period. She would obviously not take part in any investigation where physical violence could be anticipated, but she would certainly be able to trace, serve process, keep observations and even act as a witness in a civil or criminal case. However there is one very important point that many spare-time employees never seem to consider. All investigation work is extremely important, usually being carried out on behalf of the legal profession, and it must not be lightly regarded as just a means to make money. They must possess an absolute loyalty to the agency—certainly matching that of their full-time work—and realize from the very first that they may be expected to be on call any night, weekend or public holiday. Also on occasions they will have to work into the early hours, irrespective of regular employment. It might be unfortunate for someone making an early start, but if they are not prepared to accept these terms, then even the application for a job would be a waste of time.

Remuneration is very good, particularly when better assignments are being dealt with. It is not possible to give exact figures, but the employee would be paid in relation to the local charges of the agency and possibly with traces and process he might be paid on results.

Despite the fact that an employee is working on a part-time basis, the result of his labours cannot wait. The agency must know quickly everything which has occurred. Therefore, reports, traces or processes must be taken to the office the following day, possibly during the part-timer's lunch break and with a very urgent matter the report could be telephoned first thing in the morning. Never keep the agency waiting, as their clients may be enquiring for the results. Always try to grasp this sense of urgency, whatever matter is being dealt with. Even a simple debt tracing is important to someone, therefore it warrants the best possible attention.

The same rule regarding absolute discretion must be observed, no subject relating to the office ever being discussed with any outsider.

ETHICS

Many people have accused private investigators of being rather short on this attribute, usually without foundation.

The objects of the British Police are:

> The maintenance of Law and Order.
> Preservation of the peace.
> Protection of life and property.
> Prevention and detection of crime.

The same code could usefully be adopted by all private investigators, possibly with more emphasis on the last two. However, a code more directly applicable to private investigators might be:

> To accord ethical principles to all business.
> To maintain high standards of detective work.
> To actively participate in the prevention of crime.
> To guard the public against fraudulent dishonesty.
> To act in accordance with the law.

The above can be broken down into the following rules by which all private investigators should abide:

1. Never discuss a case with anyone except the client or instructing solicitor.
2. Do not accept instructions from both sides.
3. When giving evidence, always speak the absolute truth, never 'gild the lily' or 'add a bit'.
4. You owe your client absolute loyalty and must use every just and honest method on his behalf, although his payment should never influence you to go beyond these bounds, and in spite of the fee your investigations should be conducted with a careful impartiality.
5. Remember that the court does not require to hear revolting pornographic accounts, therefore there is no need to become a 'Peeping Tom'. The two essentials to be proved in a case of adultery are Opportunity and Inclination.
6. Unless ordered to do so by the judge or magistrate, never reveal the name of an informant.
7. Charge fairly and never try to make a small assignment into anything else.
8. Always aim for perfection in all cases; even then mistakes will sometimes be made, but any lower standard will guarantee calamity.
9. Deal with enquiries competently and swiftly, with a letter or interim report where delays are encountered. Never put any matter on one side if it becomes too involved. Complete it somehow, however difficult.
10. Whatever the provocation, a private investigator should never under any circumstances give way to anger.
11. There will invariably be occasions when well-founded prejudice will be felt against some party, but this must not be allowed to influence the investigator in his subsequent actions.
12. Never become even remotely involved in any shady dealings or try to 'ride the fence', i.e. always just on the edge of the law but never breaking it.
13. Avoid unnecessary disbursements for overnight accommodation if an early start would suffice. This applies equally to all other forms of expenses.
14. Do not use the occupation of private investigator to suggest greater authority by implying a police or court connection. This is an offence, but is also completely unnecessary.
15. Britain is a democratic country and in spite of a duty to the client, always bear this fact in mind with regard to invasion of privacy and restriction of personal liberty.
16. Where arrest is considered, be absolutely certain that the necessary authority exists and even if there is a clear power of

arrest is it wise or essential to use it? (These comments would not apply to criminal types actually caught in the commission of the crime, but it would possibly apply to an otherwise respectable member of the community, with a permanent address, who was willing to make a full cautioned admission. Here an arrest would be completely pointless and dangerous.)

17. Under no circumstances whatsoever should either an original or a copy voluntary, cautioned statements relating to crime, divorce or any other type of confession, ever be given or lent to a private client for they may be used in distasteful or unlawful ways, not remotely connected with fair play and justice. Inform the client of the relevant contents, but only give them to either the solicitors involved or the police. This should apply to ALL cautioned statements, even if the client is a well respected businessman. The fact that he is paying for the statements—and this is sometimes the argument—does not affect this rule.

18. The private investigator should always conduct himself with quiet decorum and never incur financial liabilities beyond his means.

19. Never reveal information to persons purporting to act as agent for the client, unless their bona fide has been checked. (This also applies to all telephone conversations; always make certain that you are speaking to an authorized person.)

16
Conclusion

The need for an adequate police force was recognized in 1829 and after several commissions had reported on the policing of London the then Home Secretary, Sir Robert Peel, formed the Metropolitan Police Force by an Act of Parliament. This is how the nicknames 'Bobby' and 'Peeler' came into use.

The occupation of private investigator has an equally old tradition, although perhaps not quite as respectable. Certainly it goes back to the reign of Queen Victoria (1837–1901) and almost certainly before these dates, as it would appear that the Metropolitan Police Force was really formed to supplant the existing and unsatisfactory system of police work by private investigators, and others, which was in operation at that time. It would therefore appear that we have an even earlier history than the Police Service; thus, even if the original investigators were not too virtuous in their dealings, today's detective can at least be proud to be a member of a traditional profession dating back to such early times.

Nowadays, a far more respectable type of person is entering the private investigation field, and the responsibility for the maintenance of higher standards together with the ability to improve them even more in the future, lies firmly at the door of newcomers. The aim should be to weed out all the unscrupulous and incompetent private investigators, replacing them with men and women of honesty and integrity, who possess the theoretical knowledge and the practical application essential to conduct such a skilful and demanding job. But before reaching this idyllic stage, a tremendous amount could be accomplished by control and licencing by the local police or local authority. This may not stop incompetence, but it would at least ensure exclusion of the fraudulent operator.

To run a detective agency is a most exacting task, requiring a strong constitution and the ability to work at constant high pressure, sometimes for weeks on end without any noticeable break. However, it is not really the work which causes the damage but more the nerve-racking, urgent nature of important enquiries, where success is so dependent on handling the whole operation in exactly the right manner. Obviously, the easy answer is simply not to get personally involved, but this attitude is very difficult to attain because unless one is completely engrossed in a difficult case, the solution may elude discovery.

There are many agencies in the country which are quite capable of dealing with straightforward enquiries, but the real test comes when a difficult assignment is encountered, depending entirely on the capabilities of the individual investigator. It is on these cases that an agency builds a good or bad reputation. Irrespective of the final result, if it is obvious from the interim and final reports that every possible angle has been explored with both intelligence and energy, then even a failure will not be a disgrace and nobody will accuse the agency of incompetence.

Should an investigator be fortunate enough to receive instructions entailing travel abroad, always make sure that at least a retainer to cover expenses has been deposited and the cheque cleared before departure. This may not apply in the case of very large companies, but is a safeguard which is always worthy of consideration. If certain undefended divorce actions happen to clash with the investigator's absence, affidavits for each testimony may, in these extenuating circumstances, be allowed by the court.

One great fault to avoid is being constantly preoccupied with money and fees. Strangely enough, this type of attitude prevents the investigator from being successful. This is possibly because he is thinking too much about money and not enough about work, concentrating only on the better paid assignments; whereas the investigator who adopts the regular habit of leaving the office on both large and small enquiries, finds that all matters are constantly up to date. The agency is, therefore, regarded as efficient and a natural prosperity ensues.

A self-employed private investigator is constantly at the beck and call of his clients, and it would be both fallacious and a complete misnomer to describe him as his own boss or master. Every client, whether solicitor or private, has the right, within reasonable limits, to expect efficiency, prompt service, individual loyalty and absolute secrecy. In one sense these people are really the employers for they supply both the work and the income; the investigator would be very wise to remember this.

To be really efficient as an investigator it is not necessary to spend hundreds of pounds on 'cloak and dagger' equipment, but a good car is fairly essential and if a second vehicle is kept, a van would be useful for observations and other duties. A well trained dog can often be employed effectively for difficult process serving, various escort duties, and makes an admirable companion for a night-long vigil on suspected premises. It is also necessary to be on good terms with the local police, as with all other local government departments.

According to some biased critics this occupation is both dishonourable and distasteful, but only a very small minority of investigators warrant this slur. Neither of these adjectives apply to the hard working investigator visualized in this book. His or her life consists of carrying out assignments on behalf of wronged clients and attempting to trace the culprit concerned, or proving an offence, so that the guilty party can be dealt with according to law. The rest of his duties consist mainly of routine process serving, tracing bad debtors, giving testimony in court and other matters mostly connected with the law. In view of this definition, policemen, bailiffs, sheriffs and all other officers carrying out the law could be similarly described! Admittedly this job is not suitable for the squeamish, unworldly individual, but like many other occupations or professions each firm should be judged on its individual merits, not collectively on the worst examples. If the investigator carries out his duties in a proper manner, the employment is both useful, honourable and also a very necessary and indispensable social service to the community.

Finally, always remember to keep your passport available and be prepared to quit the country instantly, to deal with all those 'James Bond' assignments which are sure to come along!

Now, good-bye, good luck and good hunting.

Index

Accidents, industrial, 42–7
Administration, business, 111–15
Adultery, 37, 57–70
  instructions, investigator's, 57–8
  interview notes, 62–3
  observation of, 65–7
  reports of, 63–4
  proof of, 57
  statements, 34, 63
    confession, 60–1, 67–8
    contents, 58–9
    evidence, 57
    file, 58–9, 60, 63
  see also Divorce; Matrimonial enquiries
Advertising, 14, 110, 112
Agencies, 20
  fees to, 16
Alarms, burglar, 86–7
America, 20

Boardroom security, 87
Britain, 20

Cautions, 36–8, 56, 67
  short, 33, 37–8

Clients, finding, 14, 110
Conduct money, 103–4
Confessions, 33–5, 48, 55–6, 60–1, 67–8, 70, 118
Correspondence, 113–14, 117
Court procedure, 90–1, 94–5
Criminal investigations, 14, 71–8
  dishonesty,
    salesman, 76–7
    shop manager, 73–6
    factory larceny, 77–8
  instructions in, 72–3

Debt tracing, 15, 22–5, 110, 115, 116, 121
Detective associations, 15
Dishonesty,
  factory larceny, 77–8
  salesman, 76–7
  shop manager, 73–6
Divorce, 19, 37, 91, 120
  statements, 68–9, 118
  see also Adultery; Matrimonial enquiries
Dogs, guard, 83, 89

Employees, investigator's, 111–13

Espionage, industrial, 79–80, 84
Ethics, professional, 116–18
Evidence, 96–101
   giving, 90–5
   leading questions and, 101
   privilege and, 100–1
   types of, 96–9

Fences, security of, 84
Floodlights, in security, 84

Handwriting, 39, 48–9, 98
Holidays, annual, 114

Income Tax, 114
Informants, paid, 78
Interpreters, 52–4
Interviews and interrogation, 32–5, 37

Larceny, factory, 77–8
Law firms,
   investigator and, 13–14, 15, 23, 25, 43, 57, 90, 102, 106, 108, 109, 110, 117, 118
Law studies, investigator's, 109–10
Legal process, service of, 13, 14, 102–6, 115, 121
Libel, 15
Locks, security of, 85, 87
London, 18, 20

Matrimonial enquiries, 14, 17, 21, 33, 34, 47–8, 108, 111;
   see also Adultery; Divorce
Missing persons, tracing, 14, 22, 26–31, 111

Office, investigator's, 108–9

Patrols, security, 84–5
Petitions, 49–51
Peel, Sir Robert, 119
Photographs, 43, 45, 47–8, 58, 82, 88, 97
Pinkerton, Allen, 20
Pinkerton's Agency, 20
Police, 53, 68, 70, 73, 76, 77, 88, 90, 119, 121
   ethics, 116
   investigator and, 11–12, 13, 112–13
   notebook, 63, 91
Private investigator,
   agency work and, 16
   commencing business, 107–18
   court procedure and, 90–1, 94–5
   criticisms of, 21
   ethics, 116–18
   history of, 19–21, 119
   law firms and, *see* s.vv.
   mistakes, rectifying, 14
   offences by, 15, 34
   part-time, 7–8, 13, 21, 115, 116
   police and, 11–12, 13, 112–13
   qualifications, 11, 12–14, 71, 108, 119–21
   remuneration, 8, 12, 13, 16, 19, 21, 22, 25, 30, 31, 57–8, 70, 115–16, 117, 120

woman as, 8, 12, 115
work,
  hours, 12, 115
  scope, 13, 14

Report, writing, 15

Safes, security of, 85
Security, 14, 81–9
Slander, 15, 72
Statements,
  adultery, *see* s.v.
  cautioned, 34, 37, 45, 55, 56, 78, 118
  confessions, *see* s.v.
  crime, 54–6, 70

divorce, 68–9, 118
illiterate persons, 51–2
interpreter and, 52–4
negative, 49
voluntary, 34, 37, 45, 53, 55, 118

Tracing enquiries, 15, 22–5, 110, 115, 116, 121

Wage collection, security of, 87–8, 89
Walls, security and, 84
Windows, security and, 85–6
Witnesses, 99–100
  conduct money, 103–4